TEXTILE COLLECTIONS OF THE WORLD
VOLUME 3—FRANCE

FRANCE. 16th-Century embroidered hanging on satin and velvet, 38 cm. high. *Musée des Arts Décoratifs, Paris—4383 (1143).*

TEXTILE COLLECTIONS OF THE WORLD

FRANCE. *L'Offrande à l'Amour*, Toile de Jouy by Huet, c. 1810. *Musée des Arts Décoratifs, Paris—17530 (2991 Bis).*

VOLUME 3 — FRANCE

AN ILLUSTRATED GUIDE TO TEXTILE COLLECTIONS IN FRENCH MUSEUMS

EDITOR: CECIL LUBELL

VNR **VAN NOSTRAND REINHOLD COMPANY**
NEW YORK   CINCINNATI   TORONTO   LONDON   MELBOURNE

FRANCE. Border of sculptured velvet on yellow satin, Empire period (1804–15). *Mobilier National—GMMP 756 (5567).*

Van Nostrand Reinhold Company Regional Offices: New York   Cincinnati   Chicago   Millbrae   Dallas

Van Nostrand Reinhold Company International Offices: London   Toronto   Melbourne

Copyright © 1977 by Cecil Lubell. Library of Congress Catalog Card Number 77-1628

Book and jacket design by Cecil Lubell. Manufactured in the United States of America.

Published by Van Nostrand Reinhold Company, 450 West 33rd Street, New York, N.Y. 10001. Printed in the U.S.A.

Library of Congress Cataloging in Publication Data
Lubell, Cecil.
  France.

  (Textile collections of the world; v. 3)
  Includes index.
  1. Textile fabrics—France.   2. Museums—France.
I. Title.   II. Series.
NK8849.L82   746.3'944'07444   77-1628
ISBN 0-442-24894-6

FRANCE. Empire cut-velvet border. *Mobilier National—GMMP 755 (5567).*

PHOTO CREDITS. All photographs are reproduced by courtesy of the museums credited in the captions. Wherever possible the accession number is listed first, followed by the photo-negative number in parentheses.

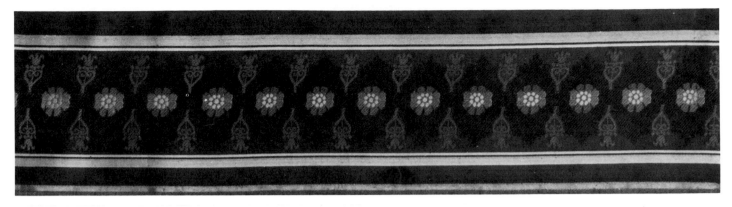

FRANCE. Empire woven-silk border in green satin with gray/white figures. *Mobilier National—GMMP 1327 (5601).*

Plan and Purpose

This is the third volume in a series —*Textile Collections of the World.* Like all volumes in the series, it combines resource information with design ideas.

As such, it is directed primarily to professional textile designers, to producers of textiles, to all craft workers in thread, and to students of textile design.

Resource information is provided in reviews of French collections.

Textile-design ideas are presented in photographs of selected pieces from the collections reviewed. They are reproduced in B/W and color.

Photographs are arranged by country of origin. I have made no attempt to present a consecutive picture history of textile design. My purpose has been to select from each collection those pieces that I believe will have the greatest visual interest for contemporary textile designers. Thus the photographic sections reflect a personal view of the collections.

My hope in compiling these volumes is that the reviews and the photographic sampling will persuade designers to explore the collections with their own eyes and hands. The best that anyone can offer in a printed book is still no more than a weak substitute for original material and personal experience.—C.L.

Contents • Volume 3 • France

INTRODUCTION

The French have chic, no? Everybody knows that, everybody says it, the world's fashion press proclaims it daily. Legendary chic, perhaps, for it is often difficult to perceive in the provincial cities of France or in the dress of many French people, especially working people. But certainly true of Paris, where the visual impact is rich and beguiling.

The same for French textiles—rich and beguiling. Call to mind some of the important styles in the decorative arts—Rococo . . . Empire . . . Directoire . . . Regency . . . Chinoiserie . . . Louis Quatorze . . . Louis Quinze . . . Art Nouveau . . . Art Deco. All these are French names, styles originating in France and now among the most universal and the most elegant terms in the lexicon of decor. And though few textile designers were widely known by name until modern times, the names of two 18th-Century French textile designers were acclaimed throughout Europe—Philippe de Lasalle (1723–1803) and Jean Baptiste Huet (1745–1811).

Since at least the 1660s French textiles have been a matter of national pride, earning the admiration of world markets and the envy of competitors in other lands. It was in 1665 that Jean Baptiste Colbert (1619–83), the shrewd finance minister to Louis XIV, organized practical government support for the country's silk-weaving industry, which had enjoyed royal patronage since the reign of Louis XI (1461–83).

Colbert's aim was to compete more successfully in world markets and to prevent the drain of French currency in expensive foreign textile imports. He had the same objective in establishing, with government support, an important lace industry at Alençon in 1661.

And he succeeded. Due to his enlightened program France quickly captured world textile leadership from Italy. The city of Lyon, building on its earlier weaving prestige, achieved international renown for the ingenuity of its designs and the supremacy of its weaving skills in silk. And all long before Joseph Marie Jacquard

(1752–1834) perfected his automated pattern loom—another notable French achievement. Even the ingenious weaving entrepreneurs of Scotland's Paisley are known to have admitted that their woven "Kashmir" shawls took second place to those of the French.

Similarly with printed textiles. The French flair for design quickly absorbed and reconstituted pattern themes found in the painted-and-printed cottons imported from India towards the end of the 17th Century. By the middle of the 18th Century French printed "Indiennes" had grown into a national symbol of fashion. In 1806 there were at least 145 textile printworks operating throughout France—among them that of Oberkampf at Jouy, possibly the most illustrious name in the long history of printed textiles. In that same year the total production of French printed cottons exceeded 5 million meters.

* * *

The products of these historic developments—French woven silks and French printed cottons—are abundantly and proudly preserved in the museums of France, together with important but less voluminous collections of two other notable French textile arts—tapestry and lacemaking. They are often exhibited hand in hand with the products of French costume art, which they supported through the centuries and which they still support with great cachet today when French couture leads the world.

In France the center of museum art is Paris, but this is only partly true of the textile arts. The country's most prestigious collection of historic woven silks is in Lyon, whose textile museum is headquarters for the Centre International d'Etude des Textiles Anciens (CIETA) an international association devoted to the study of ancient textiles. A most important record of French textile printing is in Mulhouse, long the focal point of Alsatian textile manufacturing. Both these collections are rich and rewarding as well as handsomely housed. They should be on every designer's itinerary. In the North, Tourcoing is also a key resource for its record of French woolens and contemporary Jacquards.

Still outside Paris are the great tapestries at Angers and Bayeux—both well worth a special journey. Nantes, Tours, Alençon, An-

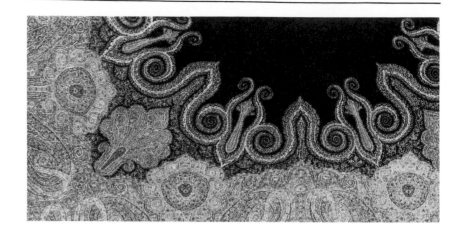

RIGHT. Detail of a French woven-wool "Cachemire" shawl produced about 1850. *Centre de Documentation des Fils et Tissus, Tourcoing—145.*

BELOW. Gold brocaded-silk border on a poppy-colored satin ground. Empire period. *Mobilier National—GMMP 246/1 (5554).*

goulème, and Strasbourg each have small specialized collections worth exploring if you are in the area. And for anyone concerned with ecclesiastical textiles the Trésor de Sens should be a rare experience.

Inside Paris the researcher in textiles faces a misery of choice. The Musée des Arts Décoratifs, when its textile collection is reorganized and given adequate exhibit space, will be the chief attraction. Its collection covers the long continuum of textile history with few gaps, and its research library is a treasure house for designers. The Louvre owns the world's outstanding collection of Coptic tapestry weaving, and its curator is the acknowledged authority in his field.

The Musée de l'Homme is perhaps the most exciting resource of all, with its large and wide-ranging collections of ethnographic textiles from the world's preindustrial cultures and its inexhaustible photographic library. The Mobilier National holds the historical record of sybaritic French palace textiles, tapestries, and rugs—many of them ancient but unused and brilliantly new. The Cluny has the unsurpassed Lady with the Unicorn tapestries and many fine examples of medieval textile art.

The Bibliothèque Forney is notable for its Art Deco and Art Nouveau textile designs; the Bibliothèque Nationale, for its Richelieu sample books and other important French textile documents. The Musée des Arts Africains et Océaniens owns a superb collection of woven and embroidered silks from Morocco, Algeria, and Tunisia, as well as fascinating appliqué panels from Dahomey. The Musée des Arts et Traditions Populaires has few flat textiles but an outstanding collection of rural French costumes and coifs. The Guimet has ancient Chinese silk fragments from the Han Dynasty.

The Musée du Costume at the Carnavalet owns examples of French costume art from 1735 to date and therefore records the changes in French apparel textiles over more than 200 years. And the same for the Centre de Documentation du Costume, with the additional attraction of fabric swatches dating back to the 18th Century and forward to the present.

These 12 Paris collections are spread out over the city, and the best way to reach them all is by way of the Metro subway system. It is

LEFT. Furnishings print by Chotard in Alsace, made in 1974. *Centre de Documentation des Fils et Tissus—1760.*

BELOW. *Les Ananas*, a woven satin designed by Charles Martin in 1923 for Bianchini Férier. *Musée des Arts Décoratifs, Paris—25978 (8103).*

fast, generally efficient, and its cars roll on rubber wheels. To this end I have listed the Metro stops for each collection and supplied a simple map showing the museum locations.

It is well to remember that all Paris museums close on Tuesdays, and some during the lunch hour. Each museum and library should be checked for opening hours. For this you should carry a copy of the monthly pamphlet issued by the Secrétariat d'Etat à la Culture. It is available without charge at the Louvre, the Hôtel de Ville, and the Hotel de Sully.

* * *

IN GRATITUDE. For special help and encouragement in assembling the materials for this volume I here record my appreciation.

To my son, Stephen Lubell, for his invaluable aid in conducting preliminary research among Paris textile collections—to Sheila Hicks, a Parisian by choice, for helping me to understand the mores of her adopted city and for opening doors that sometimes seemed impassable—to my friend, Carol Golman of Paris, for arranging advance appointments with curators—to Jacques Dupont, Inspector General of Historic Monuments, for a list of French textile collections and for his personal interest in my work—to Père du Bourguet of the Louvre, for the benefit of his knowledge and friendship—to Madame Patisson of the Musée de l'Homme Photothèque, for her remarkable goodwill and efficiency—to Nadine Gasc of the Musée des Arts Décoratifs, for compiling an inventory of her vast collection—To Monique Jay of Lyon and Nicole Delannoy of Tourcoing, for undertaking similar difficult tasks at my request—to Jacqueline Jacqué of Mulhouse, for the exemplary documentation of her notable collection—to Jean Coural and Muriel de Raïssac of the Mobilier National, for enthusiasm and encouragement warmly given when most needed—to Urline Baltrusaitis of the American Embassy in Paris, for advice and support—to the many museum staff members, named in the text, for their help in making this volume possible—and to my wife, Winifred Lubell, for her artist's eye on constant and critical questions of design.

Cecil Lubell
Wellfleet, Massachusetts
December, 1976

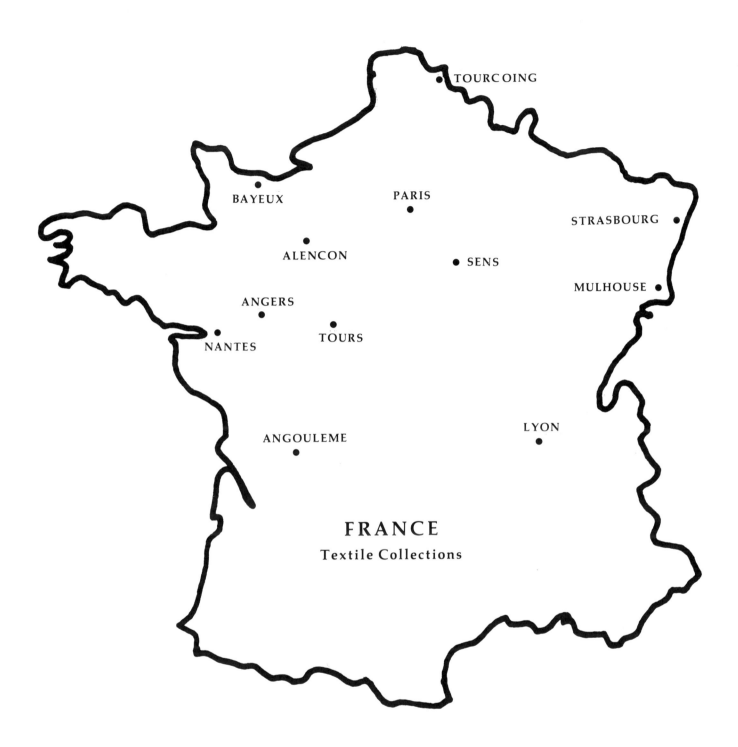

TOURCOING

BAYEUX

PARIS

STRASBOURG

ALENCON

SENS

MULHOUSE

ANGERS

NANTES

TOURS

ANGOULEME

LYON

FRANCE
Textile Collections

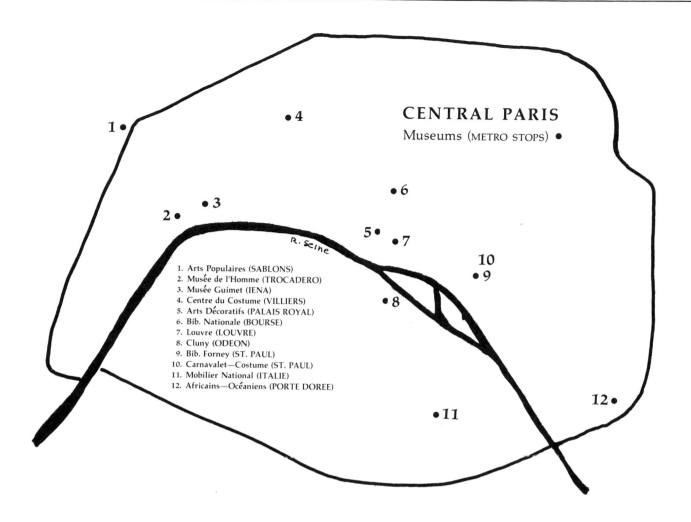

CENTRAL PARIS
Museums (METRO STOPS) •

R. Seine

1. Arts Populaires (SABLONS)
2. Musée de l'Homme (TROCADERO)
3. Musée Guimet (IENA)
4. Centre du Costume (VILLIERS)
5. Arts Décoratifs (PALAIS ROYAL)
6. Bib. Nationale (BOURSE)
7. Louvre (LOUVRE)
8. Cluny (ODEON)
9. Bib. Forney (ST. PAUL)
10. Carnavalet—Costume (ST. PAUL)
11. Mobilier National (ITALIE)
12. Africains—Océaniens (PORTE DOREE)

REVIEWS OF FRENCH TEXTILE COLLECTIONS

ARRANGED IN ALPHABETICAL ORDER BY CITY

Alençon—Musée d'Oze

Angers—Tapestry Museum

Angoulême—Musée d'Angoulême

Bayeux—Musée de la Reine Mathilde

Lyon—Musée Historique des Tissus

Mulhouse—Musée de l'Impression sur Etoffes

Nantes—Musée des Salorges

Paris—Musée des Arts Africains et Océaniens

Paris—Musée des Arts Décoratifs

Paris—Musée des Arts et Traditions Populaires

Paris—Bibliothèque Forney

Paris—Bibliothèque Nationale

Paris—Carnavalet Musée du Costume

Paris—Centre de Documentation du Costume

Paris—Musée de Cluny

Paris—Musée Guimet

Paris—Musée de l'Homme

Paris—Musée du Louvre

Paris—Mobilier National

Sens—Trésor de la Cathédrale

Strasbourg—Musée des Arts Décoratifs

Tourcoing—Centre de Documentation des Fils et Tissus

Tours—Musée des Beaux Arts

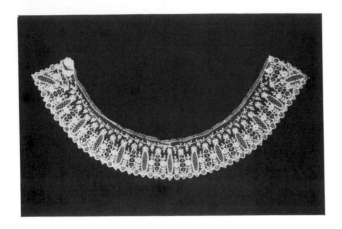

ALENCON

Musée d'Oze
Place Lamagdelaine
61000 Alençon   TEL: 26-00-97

Claude Lioult, Curator

Alençon lace is a delicate, finely structured net lace made with a needle rather than with bobbins. It originated in the city of Alençon (Normandy), but the term later became generic and was used to describe similar laces made elsewhere.

The city of Alençon became an important lacemaking center in 1661 when Colbert, Finance Minister to Louis XIV, established a factory there in order to compete with foreign laces, especially those of Italy, which were then in fashion. And it succeeded. The new lighter laces from Alençon and nearby Argentan soon became high fashion and were much in demand both in and outside of France. They became world renowned as *Point de France*.

Through the years the designs of Alençon lace changed with shifting fashion trends but the essential light net quality of the work continued, even with the advent of machine-made lace. During the 19th Century the city of Alençon still had a large and important lace industry, but this is now gone, and it is for the earlier work of the 17th and 18th Centuries that Alençon is most famous.

A record of Alençon's past fame as a lacemaking center is preserved in the city and is temporarily housed in the Hôtel de Ville and the Ecole Dentellière. The collection is not large as lace collections go, but it is a most important one in range and quality. It contains about 250 pieces and some 90 lace designs on paper. Among them are some 35 important examples recently given by Baroness Alix de Rothschild.

The laces date from the 16th to the 19th Century, for there was a cottage-lacemaking industry in the city before Colbert's venture in 1661. The major part of the collection represents 18th- and 19th-Century work. Some of the pieces are small, but a number are very large—100 inches or more in length. Most periods of French design history are represented, covering a time span of almost 400 years, with the strongest emphasis on the periods of Louis XIV, Louix XV, and Louis XVI. In addition to laces made in Alençon the collection also contains a fair sampling of work from Argentan, Bruges, Brussels, Chantilly, Cluny, England, Valenciennes, and Venice.

The lace designs on paper are all 19th-Century work made for Alençon manufacturers.

The collection of lace is under the curatorial care of the Musée d'Oze pending the creation of a new museum, which will bring the lace holdings under one roof. This is now in the planning stage.

The Musée d'Oze also owns a group of 15 textiles and costumes from Cambodia—known as the Adhémard Leclere Collection.

ANGERS

Tapestry Museum—Château d'Angers
49220 Angers   TEL: (41) 87-43-47

Antoine Ruais (prêtre), Curator

At Angers stands one of the great Châteaux of the Loire Valley, a 13th-Century feudal castle with 17 towers rising 130–160 feet in height. Within this medieval complex is a modern museum built to house the famous *Apocalypse of Angers* tapestry. Its fame is justified, for not only is this the largest tapestry in the world; it is also a great work of art.

As it now hangs in the 315-foot gallery built to house it, the *Apocalypse* measures 353 feet in length and about 14½ feet in height. It contains 67 scenes and 6 fragments on alternating red and blue backgrounds. Each scene is at least 5½ × 8½ feet, and all depict the Apocalypse of John from the Book of Revelation. Spread out among the scenes are 4 panels with "grands personnages" (plus 2 more incomplete figures held in reserve). Scholars have conjectured that the work was originally 460 × 18 feet with 84 scenes and 7 large figures, but a number of scenes have been lost due to centuries of neglect and bad treatment.

The *Apocalypse* is unquestionably the first masterpiece of medieval tapestry work, since it set the pattern for many tapestries that followed. It was commissioned by Louis I of Anjou and was woven, probably in Paris, by the most famous weaver of his time, Nicolas Bataille, between 1373 and 1379. The cartoons were drawn by the painter Hennequin of Bruges.

By the standards of any medium and of any period it is a major work of art. The detail of figures and portraiture are extraordinarily lifelike, and the total composition has a grace and excitement that sets this work apart from the many that followed in its wake. As a source of modern textile design the *Apocalypse* may be somewhat limited, but it is one of civilization's major works of art in thread and as such deserves the attention of all who concern themselves with textile art.

For those who cannot visit the Château d'Angers I can recommend the following published works on the *Apocalypse* tapestry:

1. *L'Apocalypse d'Angers.* By René Planchenault.
2. *Les Tapisseries d'Angers.* By René Planchenault.

Both volumes are well illustrated and are published by Caisse Nationale des Monuments Historiques et Sites, Grand Palais, Avenue Alexandre III, Porte G, 75008 Paris.

In addition to the *Apocalypse* in its special gallery the Château d'Angers also owns other famous tapestries of the Middle Ages and Renaissance. These are exhibited elsewhere in the château. Among the best known are Flemish works on the *Instruments of the Passion* and a mille-fleurs tapestry known as *La Dame à l'Orgue.*

ANGOULEME

Musée d'Angoulême
1, rue de Friedland
Angoulême (Charente)   TEL: 95-07-69

Robert Guichard, Curator

This museum is known for its fine ethnographic collections of African and Oceanic artifacts as well as of prehistoric archaeology. It also owns an interesting group of costumes and embroidery from Morocco—known as the Ricard Collection and exhibited in the public galleries of the museum.

In all, the Moroccan textile holdings number 109 pieces. Of these, 88 pieces are flat embroideries; the rest are garments, almost all with embroidery work.

The largest number of embroideries (80) comes from Fès.

There are also several examples of work from Rabat, Azemmour, and Midelt.

Among the embroidered costumes are robes from Tafilalet and Tetuan, as well as several pieces made in the Atlas Mountains.

BAYEUX

The Bayeux Tapestry
(Musée de la Reine Mathilde)
Ancien Evêché, rue Léonard-Leforestier
(next to the Cathedral de Notre Dame)

Mlle. Simone Bertrand, Curator

I have a long and intimate association with the Bayeux Tapestry. Like Proust's madeleine, it recalls the days of childhood. During the 1920s in my parents' Yorkshire home, company tea was served in handsome Royal Doulton china decorated with dramatic scenes from the Bayeux Tapestry. In later years I have often seen it reproduced on draperies and upholstery, on apparel fabrics for both sexes, and in a hundred books.

Surely this is not my own unique experience, for here is undoubtedly the most famous work of its kind, a medieval chanson brought to life in storybook images from a distant past.

But to know this work only in reproduction is to forego a great textile experience. When I walked into the Episcopal Palace (Ancien Evêché) at Bayeux where the tapestry now hangs, I was astonished by the clarity and freshness, the rich vibrancy, that animates this work of textile art which is now over nine centuries old (it was made about 1070 A.D.).

The fame of this masterpiece clearly rests not so much on its age as on its aesthetic. Sharply etched figures on a bleached linen ground; drawing and composition that is often primitive but has wonderful grace and movement; witty details; subtle and arresting colors; Latin captions integrated into the design, telling a story in the crisp words of an ancient ballad; intriguing small figures along the borders (7–8 cm.), echoing the illustrations for an

BAYEUX TAPESTRY Continued

oriental bestiary or Aesop's Fables, achieving the impact of imaginative drawings by children—these are the elements that make the Bayeux Tapestry a great work of art.

To see it "live" should be a rewarding experience for every designer. The journey can moreover be combined with a visit to another medieval masterpiece, Mont St. Michel—an easy drive from Bayeux.

A few facts about the Bayeux Tapestry are relevant:

1. Technique & Size. It is *not* a woven tapestry but an embroidery. It was embroidered in eight colors of wool yarn on eight varying lengths of bleached linen, which were then joined together to make a continuous frieze. The embroidery technique used was laid-and-couched work with stem and outline stitches. Its length is 230 feet and 10½ inches (70.34 cm.). Its height is 19¾ inches (50 cm.). This in itself comes as a surprise, since reproductions suggest that it is much larger in scale. Yet the smallness of the scale gives it an intimacy that is absent in larger tapestries.

2. Origin. It is *not* French work but English, or so most scholars have concluded from the internal evidence of English name spellings and a comparison with English illuminated manuscripts of the 11th Century. On this score there is still some speculation by French scholars, who seem reluctant to relinquish the provenance of this great work of art to the British.

3. Name, Purpose, & Method. The work is officially known as *La Tapisserie de la Reine Mathilde*, and the gallery in which it hangs is also known by her name. That is because it was long believed that the tapestry had been embroidered either *by* or *for* Queen Mathilde, wife of William the Conqueror and Queen of England after the Conquest.

We now know this was not so. It was commissioned by Odo, Bishop of Bayeux, half-brother to William, who was made Earl of Kent in 1067. It was perhaps destined to hang in the nave of the Cathedral at Bayeux, though this has been disputed. Queen Mathilde may, however, have helped to finance the work.

If it was made in England, as most authorities believe, it was worked by women embroiderers, probably in teams and over a two-year period. Each team would have worked simultaneously on one of the eight separate lengths before the whole was joined together.

But who was the brilliant designer? Of this there is no record. And did the embroiderers work from drawings made on the linen ground or from cartoons? Probably from drawings on the linen, but we cannot be sure.

4. Condition. The whole tapestry-embroidery is in a remarkable state of preservation. After nine centuries we should expect serious deterioration and fading of colors, but little of this is discernible in the tapestry as seen at eye level and behind glass around the walls of the Musée de la Reine Mathilde in Bayeux. True, it has been restored, but the excellent condition of the work, we are informed by French scholars, is due to the fact that it was exhibited in the Bayeux Cathedral only once a year and then for only 15 days on the anniversary of the Cathedral's dedication—a celebration that first took place on 14 July 1077 in the presence of William the Conqueror.

5. Story. In 58 captioned scenes and some 1,500 separate images the Bayeux Tapestry gives a Norman version of how Duke William of Normandy conquered England in 1066. It shows preparations for the invasion, construction of the fleet, crossing the Channel, the Battle of Hastings, and the death of King Harold of England in battle. In the course of this picture story we are given a revealing glimpse of lifestyles in the second half of the 11th Century—banqueting, taking the oath, burial, shipbuilding, navigation at sea, cavalry in the field, customs in armor, weaponry, and dress. All done with the directness of a child's painting and with great verve. No wonder school children flock to the museum in droves and examine the tapestry with great excitement.

NOTE A. Most scholars now agree that the Bayeux Tapestry was made in England and that it is the only remaining example of English embroidery before the Norman Conquest. This explains why the Victoria & Albert Museum in London owns and exhibits a hand-colored photographic facsimile of the work, made in 1871 and commissioned by the British government. Lacking the original, it displays the copy in a most ingenious manner. The reproduction is shown in a horizontal glass case outside the entrance to the museum's Textile Study Rooms (Room 107). All 230 feet of the facsimile have been rolled as a scroll, which is connected to an electric motor. At the touch of a lever the scroll unwinds under the glass and can be stopped at any given position for careful examina-

tion. Not quite as good as seeing the original but an interesting solution to the issue of national identity.

NOTE B. For those who cannot visit Bayeux or the Victoria & Albert Museum I can recommend two books on the Bayeux Tapestry, both handsomely illustrated in full color:

1. *The Bayeux Tapestry*. By Charles H. Gibbs-Smith. English text (Phaedon, 1973). Mr. Gibbs-Smith is Keeper Emeritus of the National Art Library at the Victoria & Albert Museum. He believes that the tapestry is a secular work, probably designed for the great hall of a castle rather than for the Bayeux Cathedral. This work reproduces the whole tapestry.

2. *La Tapisserie de la Reine Mathilde à Bayeux*. No. 4 in the Chefs-d'Oeuvre de l'Art series (Hachette-Fabbri-Skira, 1969). This is a large-size 40-page paperback (10½" × 14") with definitive French texts by Simone Bertrand, curator, and Henri Coulonges, art historian. Only a portion of the tapestry is reproduced.

LYON

Musée Historique des Tissus
34, rue de la Charité
69002 Lyon   TEL: 37-15-05

Jean Michel Tuchscherer, Curator
Mme. Monique Jay, Librarian

To textile curators and professionals in 33 countries on six continents the Musée Historique des Tissus is a unique and renowned institution. It is headquarters for the Centre International d'Etude des Textiles Anciens (CIETA), which publishes a bulletin twice a year and whose world-wide membership meets regularly to exchange ideas and expand its knowledge of ancient textiles.

The museum itself is elegantly housed in a 1730 mansion that was formerly the home of the Duke of Villeroy. Behind its great iron gates and cobblestoned courtyard stands a handsome three-story building with some 30 galleries devoted to permanent displays of more than 1,000 rare textiles and rugs dating from the early years of the Christian era to modern times.

Established in 1890, the museum is an outgrowth of an earlier institution—the Musée d'Art et d'Industrie—which was planned by the Lyon Chamber of Commerce in 1856 as a design aid to the city's important silk-weaving industry, which has enjoyed world-wide acclaim since the 16th Century. Its objective was to create a facility that would allow design students and professionals to study silk weaving from other parts of the world in order to increase their knowledge and develop their aesthetic tastes—and so advance the cause of Lyon silks in world markets. In 1856 France had no museum of industry, since the Musée des Arts Décoratifs in Paris was not established until 1863. French design innovation was beginning to falter, and the Lyon Chamber of Commerce was concerned to expand the horizons of Lyon's silk designers, who had brought world leadership to the industry during the 18th Century. Today the Lyon Chamber of Commerce continues this enlightened approach, and the museum is operated under its auspices.

Range of the Collection

In all, the Musée des Tissus holds about 10,000 pieces. A large number of these are not full lengths but swatches of substantial size that effectively show design motifs. The major concentration of the holdings is on silk weaving, with wide representation from the high points of silk design in Europe, Asia Minor, and the Far East.

Among the larger and more important categories in the collection are the following:

1. French silks from the 17th to the 20th Centuries, with greatest concentration on 18th-Century work from Lyon.

2. Persian and Turkish silks and velvets from the 14th to the 19th Centuries.

3. Japanese and Chinese silks, brocades, and embroideries of the 16th to 19th Centuries.

4. Italian, Sicilian, and Spanish silks from the Middle Ages to the 18th Century.

5. An important collection of ecclesiastical vestments from France, Italy, Spain, Germany, and England, covering a period from the 15th to the 19th Centuries.

6. Fine Persian carpets of the 16–17th Centuries.

7. One of the world's major collections of Coptic tapestry fragments from Egypt.

8. A representative collection of French costume from the 18th and 19th Centuries.

LEFT. Detail from a brocaded silk, Italy, 18th Century.
Musée Historique des Tissus, Lyon—28286.

RIGHT. Detail from a compound silk, Japan, 19th Century.
Musée Historique des Tissus, Lyon—23415/223.

FAR RIGHT. Velvet ikat from Persia, 17–18th Century.
Musée Historique des Tissus, Lyon—25378.

LYON Continued

9. Hundreds of silk pattern books, strongest in the period 1900 to 1925.

10. Very early examples of Sassanian, Byzantine, and Fatimid silks from the 5th Century forwards.

These are the major groupings that form the bulk of the collection and have given the Musée des Tissus its world reputation. Other and smaller categories held by the museum will be noted later.

Size of the Collection

No complete inventory of the collection has been made since 1902 when the holdings were much smaller than they are today. An extensive catalog was published in 1929, but it dealt only with the principal pieces on exhibit in the public galleries and not with the reserve collection. I wish therefore to express my gratitude to Monique Jay, who undertook the difficult task of inventorying the whole collection for this report. Her listing of the reserve collection follows:

France—Louis XIII–XVI (1610–1792)	1,963 pieces
France—Empire to Modern (1804 to date)	1,047
Spain, Italy, Sicily—10–18th C.	1,477
Far East & India—18–19th C.	1,429
Egypt & Coptic—2–8th C.	1,110
Ecclesiastical—14–20th C.	544
Persia & Asia Minor—14–19th C.	331
French Costume—18–19th C.	223
Embroidery (Civilian)—16–20th C.	542
TOTAL IN RESERVE	8,666

These figures represent only the reserve study collections. To this total Mme. Jay adds 1,100 pieces now on exhibit in the museum's public galleries. They fall within the different categories listed below. This brings the total to 9,766 pieces.

Included within the 8,666 total for the reserve collections is a miscellaneous but most important group of about 500 pieces, including very early Sassanian, Fatimid, Byzantine, and Peruvian textiles as well as later commemorative pieces (Tissus Anecdotiques), Velours Grégoire, and Toiles de Jouy.

Finally, there is a small but important collection of lace that has never been counted or classified.

This skeleton listing requires further elaboration in order to document the wide historical range and richness of this collection. To Mme. Jay's tabulation I therefore add the following notes, some of them based on the museum's 1929 catalog.

French Silks. Every important period and style in French silk design is covered in the collection. The high points include: Louis XIII, Louis XIV, Regency, Louis XV, Chinoiserie, Décor à Dentelle (lace weaves), Louis XVI, Philippe de Lasalle (designer, 1723–1803), Directoire, First Empire, all facets of 19th-Century design. The largest groups represent work from the Louis XV period (1715–74), by Philippe de Lasalle, and Lyon silks of the 18–19th Centuries. There are also important pieces of velvet, embroidery, hangings, and ecclesiastical vestments.

Spain. Work from both Catholic and Islamic Spain is well represented in the collection. There are a number of Mudéjar weavings (Moorish influence) of the 15th Century. The Hispano-Moresque style is also well covered in silks from the 10th to the 14th Centuries. In addition to silks and brocades the Spanish textiles also include many examples of cut velvet, embroidery, and elaborately worked ecclesiastical vestments.

Italy. Silks from Italy cover more than 700 years—from the 12th to the 18th Centuries. They include elaborate brocades and cut velvets from the weaving centers of Lucca, Venice, Florence, Genoa, and Sienna.

Sicily. Silks from Sicily also cover a long time span from the 10th to the 16th Centuries. Many of them come from the great weaving center at Palermo and some reflect the design influence of the Arab conquerors who ruled Sicily from 827–1070 and set up royal Tiraz workshops to produce ornate silks in the Islamic style.

Far East & India. The largest number of pieces in this category comes from Japan and China, with major concentration on 18th- and 19th-Century work. From India comes a smaller group of painted-and-dyed cottons that influenced the powerful 18th-Century French vogue for printed "Indiennes."

Egypt & Coptic. This important and exciting collection of over 1,000 pieces includes the most ancient textiles in the museum. Among them are plain linen mummy wrappings that date from as early as 3500 B.C. and tapestry

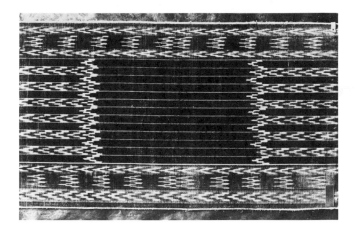

weaves from excavations at Antinoë, Akhmin, and Thebes dated at the beginning of the Christian Era. They also include some of the finest and best-preserved Coptic tapestry pieces held by any museum and compare favorably with those in the great Louvre collecton (*see Color Section*).

Ecclesiastical. As already noted, the 544 woven and embroidered pieces in this category cover almost 700 years (14–20th Centuries), with representation from France, Italy, Spain, Germany, and England. The strongest concentration dates from the 15–16th Century.

Persia & Asia Minor. Many of the 331 pieces in this group are intricate brocades and cut velvets from important weaving centers in Persia and Asia Minor. There is good representation of Turkish silks from the 16–17th Centuries. There are also several "Polish" sashes, made for Polish princes and originally woven in Persia.

French Costume. The 223 costumes in this category include both male and female ensembles dating from the reign of Louis XIV (1643–1715) through the Directoire and Empire periods. They therefore document the course of French fashion over 150 years and show many types of elaborately woven silks, metallic brocades, embroideries, and painted cottons.

Embroidery (Civilian). Some of the most elaborate work in this category comes from the early years of the 19th Century and was made for men's coats and waistcoats. There are also many other examples of French embroidery skill covering 500 years (16–20th C.).

The **miscellaneous** group of 500 pieces are included in other categories (Egypt, Persia, etc.) and are not separately classified in Mme. Jay's tabulation, but they warrant special attention. The following notes should be of interest.

Sassanian. The Sassanian Dynasty ruled Persia, Mesopotamia, Syria, and Egypt from 226–641 A.D. when Persia was conquered by the Arabs. This period was a high point in the history of silk weaving, with important textile centers at Raiy, Merv, and Gorgan. A dominant motif in the patterning was the medallion, often filled with the stylized figures of fantastic beasts and birds. These motifs are reflected in the museum pieces.

Byzantine. The more formalized patterns of Byzantine silks began to emerge in 330 A.D. under the Roman Emperor Constantine, who built his capital at Constantinople (now Istanbul). Royal textile workshops were set up here and produced boldly scaled geometric designs in woven silks. These too can be seen in the museum pieces, which date from the 5th to the 10th Centuries.

Fatimid. The Fatimid Dynasty ruled areas of North Africa (including Egypt) from 907–1171. A small group of silk textiles produced during this period is owned by the museum.

Peru. The museum owns a token group of Peruvian weavings.

Tissus Anecdotiques. These are commemorative textiles, either woven, embroidered, or printed. They were made during the end of the 18th to the end of the 19th Centuries. They celebrate historical events or famous people of the period. There are about 70 pieces in the group.

Velours Grégoire. An unusual group of about 30 velvet hangings produced by Gaspard Grégoire during the first third of the 19th Century in Aix-en-Provence. M. Gregoire developed a technique that involved coloring the yarns before they were woven into velvet cloth. The patterns are elaborate. They include such subjects as the Virgin and Child (after Raphael), portraits of Napoleon, Pope Pius VII (after David), Louis XVI, and Charles X, as well as panels of flowers, birds, and butterflies.

Toiles de Jouy. Textiles at the Musée des Tissus are predominantly woven and seldom duplicate the printed French fabrics that are so ably documented at nearby Mulhouse. However, the museum does own a representative group of Toiles de Jouy in addition to the French "Indiennes" and painted Indian cottons previously noted.

Tapestries & Rugs. The tapestry collection is modest in size, but it does include about 30 examples of French, Flemish, Rhenish, and other German work from the 11th, 15th, and 16th Centuries. The rug collection, as already mentioned, is notable and is exhibited in the museum's two-story Great Hall of Carpets. In addition to 15th- and 16th-Century Persian carpets there are fine examples of rug weaving from China, Indo-Persia, and France (Savonnerie).

Lace. No count or classification of the lace collection has yet been made, but I would estimate that it holds perhaps 500 pieces. They are mainly French in origin, but there are also representative examples from other important lacemaking centers in Europe.

The Public Galleries

The 1,100 pieces exhibited in the museum's public gal-

LEFT. Sculptured velvet (dalmatic), Italy, 16th Century. *Musée Historique des Tissus, Lyon—22376.*

RIGHT. Exterior of the Musée de l'Impression sur Etoffes, Mulhouse. The museum was founded in 1858.

FAR RIGHT. One of the high-ceilinged galleries at the Musée de l'Impression sur Etoffes in Mulhouse.

LYON Continued

leries—some 30 rooms on three floors—represent textiles from all the categories listed in this report. The pieces on exhibit are generally the most important examples from each category and period. The galleries are well lit, and, though the exhibits are behind glass, the designs are clearly visible. A few highlights will serve to indicate the depth and richness of the exhibits.

● A whole gallery devoted to the silk weavings of Philippe de Lasalle, perhaps the most famous textile designer of the 18th Century.

● Six rooms with panel displays presenting a historical review of French silk weaving by style and period.

● The Great Hall of Carpets, two stories high.

● The Coptic room, with some of the most interesting and best-preserved tapestry pieces in the collection.

● The Persian room, with fine examples of elaborate silk weaving covering several centuries.

● The large Far East gallery, sometimes devoted to exhibits of contemporary fabrics.

● Four rooms displaying ecclesiastical textiles dating from the 15th to the 18th Centuries.

● The Sienna & Lucca gallery—silk weaving from Italy's important early textile centers.

● The costume gallery, with French costumes for men and women from the 18th and 19th Centuries.

● The third floor (four galleries), devoted to textiles from Spain and Italy.

The Textile Study Room

This is the main repository of the museum's reserve collections and a treasure house for designers. It is a small room near the library, but it is packed to the ceiling with about 150 large folios (some 18–24 inches in length) that contain thousands of woven samples and designs on paper. Most of the samples are large enough to show the basic pattern motif and some show full repeats.

Among the major groupings are the following:

Italy, 15–18th Century	27 folios
France, Louis XV	25
France, Louis XVI	18
Far East	13
Japanese Brocades, 18–19th Century	17
Coptic	13
Spain	5
Sonia Delaunay Designs	2
Raoul Dufy Designs	1
Décor à Dentelle	3

All these and a number of other design sources are open to the student and professional designer, with adequate facilities for uninterrupted work in the Study Room.

Photographs. The Textile Study Room also houses the museum's large collection of photographs, which covers all categories of textiles in the collection. In all there are over 3,000 black-and-white prints on file, together with several hundred color transparencies. The black-and-white prints are clearly cataloged by culture and period and provide an excellent quick review of the museum's holdings. Copies can be ordered through the museum by arrangement with a private photographer.

The Library

The library at the Musée Historique des Tissus contains a valuable specialized collection of some 6,000 bound volumes, brochures, and periodicals. It is one of the most extensive libraries in the world on the history and technology of textiles as well as on textile design. It is actively used by curators from French museums but also by curators of foreign textile collections.

It is frequently the scene of intense study sessions with curators who are seeking to identify the source or the construction or the date of a particular textile in their collection. These sessions are usually presided over by Gabriel Vial, Secretary of CIETA, who makes his headquarters in the library and is very knowledgeable on all matters related to ancient textiles. As a result the library and its unmatched resources of hard-to-find texts has become a true international center for the study of ancient textiles.

For designers its resources are equally productive. Its shelves are filled with rare volumes of an earlier era, illustrated with superb color plates of ancient textiles.

One such work on the library shelves deserves special attention—a study in 17 volumes (several are missing) on *The Textile Fabrics of India*. It was prepared by J. Forbes Watson and was published in 1872–4 by the India Mu-

seum, London. In effect these 17 volumes in themselves become a museum of Indian textile art, since they contain almost 900 swatches of the most exquisite Indian fabrics I have yet seen. The swatches are all large (4 × 7 inches), and each large swatch is supplemented by a smaller swatch of the same textile—"for examination of texture." The designs represent styles from the important textile-producing regions of India and cover work in silk, wool, cotton, muslin, and calico. For designers this one work, as the Michelin guide might say, is worth a special journey.

Publications

Catalogue des Principales Pièces Exposées. By Henri d'Hennezel (1929). This is the catalog previously noted. It contains 150 pages and 32 photographs. The text describes and dates 768 pieces of woven and embroidered textiles, rugs, and tapestries that were on exhibit at the Musée Historique des Tissus in 1929. It is available from the museum.

Les Soieries d'Art. By Raymond Cox (Hachette, Paris, 1914). This large work contains a history of silk weaving in Europe and the Far East. It is profusely illustrated with 100 black-and-white photographs of pieces in the Musée Historique des Tissus, of which Raymond Cox was Director from 1903–21. The work is out of print but can be consulted in the museum library and in other leading libraries of the world.

Postcards. The Musée Historique des Tissus has published some 15 colored postcards of important pieces in the collection.

MULHOUSE

Musée de l'Impression sur Etoffes

3, rue des Bonnes Gens
68100 Mulhouse   TEL: (89) 45-51-20

Mme. Jacqueline Jacqué, Curator

I doubt there is any institution in the world that offers the textile designer more impressive resources for print design than the Musée de l'Impression sur Etoffes (M.I.S.E.) It is not nearly as well known as it deserves to

be, and this becomes evident from the following telescoped statistics:

1. It is a museum devoted almost exclusively to printed textiles and to printing technology.

2. Its collection covers all types of printing and dyeing, by hand and machine, from the 18th Century forward—in Europe, Asia, Africa, Japan, the Pacific, and the U.S.A. It is without doubt the largest collection of its kind in the world.

3. It owns about 3,500 large examples of printed fabric, some 200,000 original print designs on paper, plus about 6,000,000 swatches of printed fabric—chiefly French—mounted in over 1,600 folios. In addition there are thousands of printer's trial proofs on paper (in full repeat), some 300 Japanese stencils, and over 11,000 examples of wallpaper design.

4. It houses a specialized library of 1,200 volumes on the history and technology of textile printing.

5. It provides exceptional facilities for studying the collection with ease and for making copies of designs either by drawing or photograph. It has a well-equipped modern photographic laboratory of professional caliber.

6. It offers the researcher a vast and comprehensive documentation on the long history of textile printing in France from 1750 to the recent past.

Collection Launched in 1833

M.I.S.E. is jointly supported by the Société Industrielle de Mulhouse, by the city government, and by the Chamber of Commerce. It also comes under the jurisdiction of the French Ministry of Cultural Affairs. Founded in 1858, it is the logical outgrowth of the important textile-printing industry of the region—one of the major industries of Alsace. (In 1869 the Haut-Rhin region produced 82 million meters of printed cloth.)

Its enormous collection of sample books was launched in 1833 when the Société Industrielle invited 42 printworks in the Haut-Rhin region to deposit examples of their annual production in an archive. This arrangement continued over the years, supplemented by private donations, always with the understanding that the company samples so deposited would not be released for public use until such time as the donor agreed to their release—but not less than 5 years or more than 50 years after the date of deposit.

Two Separate M.I.S.E. Functions

The Musée de l'Impression sur Etoffes operates on two levels:

1. The public level, whose galleries are open to the general public. Here are mounted changing exhibits of printed textiles and a permanent display of ancient and modern equipment for printing both by hand and by machine.

2. The professional level, known as the Service d'Utilisation des Documents (S.U.D.). In a study hall 100 meters square the vast collection of some 1,600 swatch folios (souches) is housed in open library stacks for easy reference. This facility is available to professionals on payment of fees, which (in 1976) ranged from 150 francs per half day to 1,000 francs per week.

Three Categories of Textile Holdings

The total collection at M.I.S.E. is arranged in three separate categories as follows:

1. Exotic & Oriental Textiles. These are all pieces of craftwork, many very large, made entirely by hand and originating outside of Europe.

2. Western Prints. European and American printed textiles from the 18th to the 20th Century, made both by hand and by machine.

There are about 3,500 pieces in these two categories, and several hundred of them are always on display in the large public galleries of the museum. From time to time these displays are changed. During my visit the exhibit included printings and dyeing from India, Persia, S.E. Asia, and, of course, France.

3. The S.U.D. Collection. This is a vast range of some 6,000,000 swatches, trial proofs, original designs, and wallpapers dating from 1750 to the present and originating chiefly in France.

A more detailed description of these three categories follows:

1. Exotic & Oriental Collection

The following table shows a statistical breakdown of the holdings in this category—totaling about 600 pieces.

TECHNIQUE	SOURCE	DATES	NO. OF PIECES
Painted & Dyed	Persia, Indies	18–20 C.	160
Plangi	Africa, Japan, Indies	19–20 C.	40
Batik	Indonesia, Africa	19–20 C.	70
Ikat	Iran, Cambodia, Japan	19–20 C.	13
Tapa	Polynesia	19 C.	15
Stencils	Japan	19 C.	300

Though this category in the collection is not large and is somewhat limited in depth, it includes a number of exceptionally fine pieces. Among them are a distinctive 18th-Century Indian painted-and-dyed palampore from Rajistan; a 1780 painted-and-dyed cover from Persia, formerly belonging to the Shah Aga Mohammed; large and superb examples of ikat work from Cambodia (see Color Section); and a major collection of 19th-Century Japanese printing stencils, many of them reinforced with structures of human hair.

2. Western Prints

Most western countries known for their textile prints are modestly represented in this category—with the exception of Scandinavia. The major documentation, however, is understandably concentrated on French work. A statistical breakdown follows:

SOURCE	18 C.	19 C.	20 C.	KERCHIEFS	TOTAL
France (general)	69	178	18	149	414
Jouy	191	112		30	333
Nantes	114	68		1	183
Bordeaux	24	18		1	43
Rouen	26	88		120	234
Alsace	178	407	42	98	725
England	76	130	5	163	374
U.S.A.	3	73	8	31	115
Italy	1	30	16	20	67
TOTAL	682	1,104	89	613	2,488

This adds up to about 2,500 pieces. An additional 1,000 or so pieces represent smaller French producing centers such as Marseilles, Valence, Tarare, etc., as well as the foreign countries of Switzerland, Germany, Holland, and the U.S.S.R.

Of the pieces listed in the above table the largest number are toiles, whose subjects are historical, mythological,

LEFT. Two more views of the spacious galleries at the Musée de l'Impression sur Etoffes in Mulhouse.

RIGHT. A section of the study hall at the Musée de l'Impression sur Etoffes, Mulhouse. The vast documentation of French textile printing from 1750 forward is contained in some 1,600 swatch portfolios like those shown here.

and pastoral. Most are in a fine state of preservation and reveal the major trends in toile design through the 18th and 19th Centuries.

The **Jouy** pieces are especially noteworthy, since they include many examples of work by Oberkampf's leading designer Jean-Baptiste Huet (1745–1811), among them the famous *Les Travaux de la Manufacture* (1783), which illustrates the whole process of textile printing at the Oberkampf works. Also in the group are representative toiles by other designers who followed Huet at Jouy— Pinelli, Hem, and Hippolyte Lebas. In addition there are several women's costumes made of Oberkampf toiles.

The **Nantes** group has a large number of pieces from the famous printworks of the Petitpierre family, which operated from 1760 to 1866. Among them is the brilliantly colored toile *Toilette de Vénus* (see Color Section).

From the **Bordeaux** region come examples of work from the J. B. Meillier printworks at Beautiran.

The **Rouen** group is notable chiefly for its printed kerchiefs by such designers as Buquet (father and son) and from such manufacturers as P. Bataille of Deville, E. Renault of Darnetal, and Lamy-Godart. These are chiefly commemorative kerchiefs with historical themes.

From **Alsace** comes the largest and best-documented collection of 725 pieces. In 1836 there were 40 important printworks in the region and all are represented in the collection. Among them are the following: Haussmann Frères of Logelbach (near Colmar), Senn Bidermann & Cie of Wesserling, Jean Koechlin of Mulhouse, Scheurer-Lauth of Thann, Koechlin Baumgartner et Cie of Lörrach, Maison Thierry-Mieg, Ch. Steiner of Ribeauvillé, Maison Schwartz-Huguenin of Mulhouse, Maison Koechlin Ziegler, and Manufacture Hartmann of Munster.

A detailed and illustrated description of this Haut-Rhin collection can be found in two books written by the two previous curators of M.I.S.E. Both were published by F. Lewis, Leigh-on-Sea, England. They are: *The Fabrics of Mulhouse & Alsace 1750-1800* by Elisabeth Albrecht-Mathey (1968) and *The Fabrics of Mulhouse & Alsace 1801-1850* by J. M. Tuchscherer (1972).

From **Great Britain** comes an interesting group of toiles in pastoral, historical, and sporting themes as well as a large group of commemorative kerchiefs. Early work by Robert Jones at Old Ford and Talwin & Forster at Bromley Hall are both represented, as well as more recent by artists Ben Nicholson and Henry Moore.

From the **U.S.A.** comes a modest but interesting group of 115 pieces, chiefly 19th-Century work. Among them are patchwork quilts of printed fabrics and a series of documentary prints on historical subjects such as the portraits of U.S. presidents and events in the life of George Washington.

From **Italy** the most interesting pieces are printed shawls made in the district of Liguria. Decorated with motifs of trees and flowers, they were part of the traditional costume of the region in the first quarter of the 19th Century. Also in the Italian group is a series of kerchiefs illustrating festival days and historical themes.

Engel-Dollfus, Becker, & Holden Collections

A major part of the 3,500 pieces held in the public sector of M.I.S.E. came to the museum in three separate collections.

The Engel-Dollfus Collection was presented in 1872 by F. Engel-Dollfus. It contains many of the more ancient pieces held by M.I.S.E.

The Louis Becker Collection came to the museum in 1954. It was assembled by the Paris couturier Louis Becker (1882–1949), who traveled widely to indulge his passion for rare textiles. It contains 711 pieces of painted or printed toile and 484 kerchiefs. The collection is extremely well documented and the principal sources of the work are: Agen, Angers, Augsburg, Bordeaux, Bourges, Jouy, Montpellier, Nantes, and Neuchâtel. The Becker fabrics have been exhibited several times at M.I.S.E.—with accompanying catalogs.

The Agnes J. Holden Collection was acquired by M.I.S.E. in 1961. Ms. Holden was an American who studied in France and spent thirty years assembling printed fabrics used in the home. From 1930 to 1959 the collection was exhibited several times in New York City, and the museum owns catalogs of these earlier exhibits. The collection consists of 625 large examples of fine printwork from Alsace, Jouy, Nantes, Bordeaux, Rouen, Great Britain, Persia, and the U.S.A. It also includes a famous commemorative kerchief illustrating the signing of the Declaration of Independence.

The S.U.D. Collection

The Service d'Utilisation des Documents (S.U.D.) was established by the museum as a separate research facility

LEFT. 18th-Century costumes of printed fabrics on exhibit at the Musée de l'Impression sur Etoffes, Mulhouse.

RIGHT. Block-printing demonstration in the Gallery of Techniques, Musée de l'Impression sur Etoffes, Mulhouse.

FAR RIGHT. A pantograph machine for engraving designs on rollers, also in the Gallery of Techniques, Mulhouse.

MULHOUSE Continued

for professional textile designers and producers. It is housed in a high-ceilinged study hall about 100 meters square whose walls are stacked with large folios crammed with examples of printwork and original designs dating from 1750 forwards. Dates are clearly visible of the folio spines so that it is possible to select and use the folio of any given year or period.

The total number of folios currently stands at about 1,600, and they contain upwards of 6,000,000 examples. Of this total 382 folios are devoted to original designs on paper (about 200,000 pieces), and the vast remainder to fabric swatches (close to 6,000,000), trial proofs in repeat (several thousand), and wallpapers (over 11,000).

Most of the work is French in origin, but there are also interesting examples from Great Britain, the U.S.S.R., Japan, and Germany.

From a collection so vast it is impossible here to mention more than a few highlights to indicate the richness of the source material. These have been selected by the curator, Mme. Jacqué, and are listed below, together with the folio numbers:

● An early folio (No. 781) containing some 4,000 samples of French work from 1790–1793. Gift of J.-M. Haussmann.

● Four folios with 632 examples of work dating from 1760–1808 (No. 514) and 1777–1852 (No. 788). Gift of the Société Industrielle.

● 564 examples of "Indiennes" printing dated 1795 (No. 1368.T.1). Gift of Mme. Paul Ziegler.

● 55 examples of printwork from Iran and the Indies dating from the end of the 18th and the beginning of the 19th Century (No. 1494).

● From 1800–1929 a vast range of samples that document the innovations in textile chemistry and printing technique. They include a special group (Prud'hommes) covering home and fashion fabrics for the years 1829–1882.

● Valencias—printed wool-silk fabrics from 1820–30 (No. 220.2).

● 19th-Century printed shawls on grounds of Adrianople Red, for which Mulhouse printworks became famous (967.195.1).

● Almost 5,000 examples of extremely fine chrome-yellow printing produced by Nicolas Koechlin Frères from 1819–1828 (No. 228.1).

● Printed-silk foulards from 1873–79—1,700 examples (Nos. 316–323).

● Waistcoat prints from 1858–70—4,800 examples (Nos. 338–340).

● Ribbons of many kinds. One folio (No. 999) from 1907–1909 contains 3,900 examples.

● Sample books of cotton printing from Rouen manufacturers in the years 1858–1880 (Nos. 376–379)—8,280 samples.

● Over 7,000 examples of Nantes printwork, many from the famous house of Favre Petitpierre (Nos. 171–180).

● Over 10,000 samples of British printing covering the periods 1835–36, 1845–50, 1849–52, 1853–55, and 1900–1903. They include work from Dalglish Falconer of Manchester and Glasgow, Thomas Hayle of Manchester, and others (Nos. 1459, 138–143, 920, 921, 893).

● From the U.S.S.R. a group of 80 examples printed by Emile Zundel of Moscow in 1876 and another 100 examples of Russian printwork produced about 1912 (Nos. 965.3.1, 1327, 1328).

● A Japanese folio with 183 samples of printwork made about 1920 either in Tokyo or Kyoto (956.12.1).

● A German folio of 1,800 samples from the years 1905–6 (No. 941).

● About 60 folios of wallpapers containing more than 11,000 examples of French design work covering the years 1850–1900 (Nos. 247–50, 547, 1043–51, 961–989, 660–666).

● Several thousand trial proofs of printing plates—full-repeat strikeoffs on paper. A large number of these are intricate and beautifully articulated Alsatian "Paisley" designs from the mid-19th Century. Another large group of 629 designs are 18th-Century British copperplate strikeoffs from such famous houses as Talwin & Forster of Bromley Hall, Nixon & Co. of Phillipsbridge, Robert Jones of Old Ford, and the firms of Munns, Ware, and Nash (Nos. 381–3, 1487–9).

200,000 Print Designs on Paper

The major collection of print designs on paper held by M.I.S.E. has recently been made the subject of a study by Prof. Bernard Jacqué of the Ecole des Beaux-Arts in Mul-

house. The study was published in Bulletin No. 761 of the Société Industrielle de Mulhouse (April 1975).

The period covered by Prof. Jacqué's inventory is 1777–1900, for which he has tabulated the holdings by date, region, and designer or manufacturer. The total is over 200,000 pieces. The largest number of designs originated in Alsace, followed by Nantes. The whole collection is a remarkably rich source of design inspiration. I am particularly impressed by the quality of the "Paisley" designs, for which Mulhouse became justifiably renowned, and by the superb painted floral designs of Mulhouse's Atelier Schaub. There are 500 of these designs in the collection (see Color Section).

Designers may also be interested in a small group of floral patterns created by photography. They were made by Adolphe Braun (1818–77), who began his career as a textile designer for Maison Dollfus-Mieg and later switched to photography.

A Specialized Textile Library

The M.I.S.E. library is a specialized one, with about 1,200 volumes on the history and technology of textile printing. It backs up the textile collection and adds further documentation where needed to the S.U.D. samples. Among the volumes are several rare manuscripts, many account books of Alsatian textile printworks, plus rare works on textile chemistry and color.

One of the library's proudest possessions is a 1766 work by Jean Ryhiner, son of Samuel Ryhiner, who introduced "Indiennes" printing to Basle about 1716–17. Jean Ryhiner's work describes the origins of India's painted-and-dyed panels as well as the whole process of producing these unique textiles, which launched the great European print vogue of the 18th Century. Another volume of great interest to designers is the work of J. Persoz, published in Paris, 1846. It is a theoretical and practical treatise on textile printing in four volumes, with 165 illustrations, 429 swatches of fabric, and 20 block prints.

Photographic Laboratory

M.I.S.E. is well equipped to serve designers with a large collection of several thousand negatives and a modern photographic laboratory directed by Louis Meyer. Contact prints and blowups of existing negatives can be made to order, and there are facilities for taking new photographs of museum pieces in color or black-and-white.

Gallery of Techniques

One large gallery at M.I.S.E. is devoted to a permanent exhibition of equipment and machinery for textile printing. The displays follow the evolution of printing techniques from the close of the 18th Century forward. It is one of the most extensive exhibits of its kind in the world and carries the visitor intelligently from woodblock to metalblock to copperplate to roller engraving by pantograph and roller printing to screen printing both by hand and by automatic machine. Demonstrations of textile printing are given in this gallery on Monday and Wednesday afternoons from May to September.

Publications

Catalogues published by M.I.S.E. include the following.

1. *Le Musée de l'Impression sur Etoffes.* An illustrated 98-page catalog of the museum holdings and its history. It contains excellent articles on printing techniques, on Toiles de Jouy, on textile chemistry and color, on the early history of European textile printing, and on the development of Mulhouse as a printing center.

2. *La Toile de Jouy—Dessins et Cartons de J. B. Huet.* By J. M. Tuchscherer.

3. *Sonia Delaunay: Etoffes Imprimées des Années Folles.*

4. *Ceintures et Costumes Polonais.* 1972 exhibit catalog.

5. *Paule Marrot.* 1973 exhibit catalog.

6. *Raoul Dufy, Créator d'Etoffes.* 1973 exhibit catalog.

7. *Soieries Chinoises.* 1974 exhibit catalog.

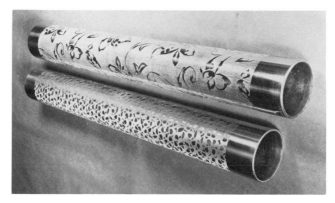

Engraved-printing rollers in the Gallery of Techniques.

NANTES

Musée des Salorges
Château des Ducs de Bretagne
44000 Nantes   TEL: 47-18-15

R. R. Chaigneau, Curator

From 1759 (when French edicts against fabric printing were withdrawn) until 1866 Nantes was an important textile-print center. Its printworks rivaled those of Jouy in the production of toiles and "Indiennes," and the name of one Nantes producer, Petitpierre, was almost as well known as Oberkampf (*Toilette de Venus*, Color Section).

The Nantes printing industry was launched by one Louis Langevin, who came to the city in 1759. He printed a wide range of fabrics, including cloths for slave-trade barter, "Persian" designs, chintz for export to Spain and Italy, and many decorative kerchiefs. His annual production was 6–7,000 pieces, and he employed up to 200 workers in his plant on the bridge of Nantes near Les Récollets on the Loire River.

By 1783 there were nine printworks in Nantes, employing 1,200 workers. Among them were the firms of Pierre Dubern, the Gorgerat Brothers (1730–1815), Kuster, Pelloutier, and the brothers Aristide and Ferdinand Petitpierre, who came to Nantes from Couvet near Neuchâtel. The Petitpierre firm was so successful that in 1785 it produced 25,000 pieces of printed cloth, many of them known as "Cameo" designs.

Subjects for Petitpierre toiles were taken from many areas. From Greek mythology came the toiles *Triumph of Amphitrite, Car of Aurora, Temple of Venus, Psyche & Love, Rape of Adonis*. From history came such toiles as *Bonaparte in Egypt, Richard the Lion Hearted*, and *Mary Stewart*. There were also rustic themes such as *The Village Bride, Lunch in the Country, The Farm*, and *The Quack*.

And many other subjects, all of which are represented in the small but representative collection of printed textiles held by the Musée des Salorges. In all there are about 200 pieces in the collection. Half of them were made in Nantes. The rest come from Jouy, Bordeaux, Montpellier, Rouen, Mulhouse, and Munster.

It should also be noted here that a substantial group of 183 Nantes prints are held by the Musée de l'Impression sur Etoffes in Mulhouse.

PARIS

Musée des Arts Africains et Océaniens
293, Avenue Daumesnil   Metro: Porte Dorée
75012 Paris   TEL: 343-14-54

Mlle. Marthe Guérard, Curator, Maghreb Art
Mme. Colette Noll, Curator, African Art
Mlle. Margerite Olagnier-Riottot, Chief Curator

Two factors make the Musée des Arts Africains et Océaniens (M.A.A.O.) an important resource for textile designers:

1. It collects and exhibits textiles as fine art—not as ethnographic documents (the province of the Musée de l'Homme).

2. It owns a superb collection of embroidered and woven silks from Morocco, Algeria, and Tunisia (Maghreb).

The museum occupies an imposing structure in the S.E. corner of Paris on the edge of the Bois de Vincennes. It was constructed in 1931 for the Colonial Exposition of that year and is considered one of the more important modern building designs from the first half of the 20th Century. The long colonnaded face of the structure is covered with a vast stone bas-relief, 13 meters high, the work of sculptor Alfred Janniot. It is one of the largest in the world and depicts the contributions of Africa, Oceania, and Asia to France as well as the symbolic figures of Abundance, Peace, and Liberty. The building also houses a tropical aquarium.

In 1960 under the sponsorship of André Malraux, then Minister of Culture, the building was given over to the present museum, which is devoted to the arts of Black Africa, North Africa (Maghreb), and Oceania. Among its other important holdings the museum owns one of the world's finest collections of African sculpture.

None of this may seem relevant to the Museum's textile collection, yet it forms an impressive background for the exhibit of textiles as art.

The Textile Collection

Between its reserve collection and its gallery exhibits the M.A.A.O. owns about 700 examples of textile art. The largest unit is Moroccan, with about 500 pieces. The

RIGHT. Example of 18th-Century Moroccan embroidery from the Musée Historique des Tissus, Lyon. Some 500 examples of similar Moroccan embroidery work are held by the Musée des Arts Africains et Océaniens in Paris. It is considered to be the largest such collection outside Morocco.

remainder is chiefly Algerian and Tunisian work, plus six large panels from Dahomey and a few pieces of tapa cloth from the Pacific area.

Representative pieces from each of these regions are on display in the public galleries. The reserve collection is not accessible, but this is not a serious deprivation. The pieces on display have been carefully selected for their visual and technical excellence. Most of the work covers a time span from the 17th to the 19th Centuries, with the best representation coming from the 18th and 19th Centuries.

Following are a few highlights from the exhibits.

Morocco. The 500 pieces in this category form what is considered to be the largest collection of its kind outside Morocco. Among those pieces on exhibit behind glass are urban embroideries and costumes from the cities of Fès, Meknès, Salé, Rabat, Tetuan, Chéchouen, and Azemmour. All the work was done by women, and most of the embroidery is silk on silk grounds, though there are some pieces on grounds of linen and cotton.

I was particularly attracted to the following Moroccan pieces:

- An embroidered curtain from Rabat, 19th Century (MNAM 1968.4.2).
- A woman's woven-silk sash from Fès, early 19th Century (MNAN 1970.4.9).
- An embroidered hanging in many-colored silk from Chéchouen, 19th Century (MNAN 1961.12.4).
- A silk-embroidered cushion from Salé, mid-19th Century (MNAM 1969.2.1).
- Another woman's silk sash from Fès, 19th-Century work (MNAM 1970.4.14).
- An embroidered bed cover from Tetuan, 18th Century.
- Several extraordinary embroidered caftans from the 18th Century, some in velvet with gold thread, others with elaborate decorations in gold braid. A few very rare pieces date from the 16th Century.

The reserve collection of Moroccan textiles also holds 10 carpets, about 25 woven silk belts or sashes, and some 15 pieces of woven wool from the coastal and mountain regions.

Algeria. The Algerian work on display is equally sumptuous, though the collection is smaller and therefore possibly less representative. Most of the pieces were embroidered by women on linen grounds, many with decora-

tions in silk, silver, and gold threads. These are largely urban costume pieces dating from the 17th to the 19th Centuries. An especially noteworthy piece is an embroidered-silk shawl from the 18th Century (MNAM 1967.11.7).

Tunisia. The exhibits from Tunisia are also chiefly women's costume pieces, both urban and rural. Again, the intricate embroidery or braided decoration is made with silver and gold thread on grounds of silk, linen, and wool. The rural work is older and reveals the traditional styles of the region. The urban pieces are later in date and reveal design influences from Turkey, Greece, and Andalusia.

Dahomey. Completely different from the Maghreb work is a series of six appliqué panels held by the Black Africa section of the museum. (A similar panel is owned by the Musée de l'Homme—see Color Section). Three of these large panels are on display. Each is about 220 by 130 cm. in size, and the appliqué work is done on silk grounds. They are historical hangings originally made in 1890 to commemorate the war of King Fon of Dahomey and other national events. The originals of these panels once hung in the Palace of Abomey but were destroyed, and those owned by the museum are replicas made in 1913 by the artisan Yemadje. A black-and-white photograph of the *King Fon* panel is available from the *Service de Documentation Photographique de la Réunion des Musées Nationaux*, 89 Avenue Victor-Hugo, 75116 Paris (*Acc. No. MNAM 1963.270; Neg. No. 68.DN.2081*).

PARIS

Musée des Arts Décoratifs
(Union Centrale des Arts Décoratifs)
Pavillon de Marsan, 107–109 rue de Rivoli
75001 Paris   TEL: 260-32-14

Mme. Nadine Gasc, Curator of Textiles
Mme. Sonia Edard, Photographic Service

The Paris Decorative Arts Museum owns what may be the largest textile collection in the world. It is in a class with the major textile holdings of London's Victoria & Albert Museum and New York's Metropolitan Museum of Art—but it has much greater depth in French textiles.

PARIS ARTS DECORATIFS Continued

Here are a few bare statistics (figures are approximate):

- About 30,000 pieces of substantial size—woven textiles, printed fabrics, stencils, embroideries, lace, tapestries, and rugs—dating from the 5th to the 20th Century.

- 6,500 swatch books containing at least 10 million samples of woven and printed fabric.

- 250 weavers' record books (livres de remettage) with some 20,000 swatches, each listing the technical details of fabric construction.

- Thousands of contemporary French textile samples, still uncounted and dating from 1960 forward.

- Over 15,000 designs on paper (mises en cartes) in 200 albums.

- About 1,500 volumes with original designs and textile printers' proofs in repeat.

- Some 15,000 swatches of trimmings for costumes and home furnishings.

- A costume collection numbering about 1,500 complete ensembles and several thousand costume accessories.

- A superb library for textile-design research.

- A school of decorative art that trains students for professions concerned with design and interior decor.

All this within the confines of a museum that occupies five floors and 125 galleries in the Pavillon de Marsan, a huge wing of the Louvre Palace complex. It is operated privately by the Union Centrale des Arts Décoratifs in space provided by the state. In its present location the museum was officially opened in 1905 after occupying other locations from the year of its foundation in 1863.

It is a museum devoted primarily (but not exclusively) to the decorative arts of France, making it possible for the student to trace the evolution of French interior architecture, furniture, and decorations from the Middle Ages to 1900.

Launched in 1863

The foundation for this vast textile collection and educational facility was laid in 1863 when the Union Centrale des Beaux Arts was launched in Paris. This later developed into the present institution, and its chief objectives were much the same as those that motivated the founders of the Victoria & Albert Museum in London and the Cooper-Hewitt Museum in New York. They sought to raise the standards of industrial design so that their manufacturers could earn a larger share of world trade.

This aim and the competitive stance of the founders was frankly and unequivocally expressed in the first resolution of the Union Centrale organizing commission. It stated: "Since the Universal Expositions of 1851 and 1862 there has been immense progress throughout Europe, and it is clear that, if we are not to remain stationary, we cannot conceal the fact that our lead has diminished, that it may even be wiped out. In spite of the success achieved by our manufacturers, it is our duty to remind ourselves that a defeat is possible, that it may not be far off, if, from now on, we do not make efforts to preserve that supremacy which cannot be maintained unless we are constantly on guard to perfect it. The British industry in particular, *very backward from an artistic point of view* [editor's italics], has made prodigious progress in a few years, ever since the Exposition of 1851, and if it continues to move at the same pace, we could soon be surpassed."

France vs. Great Britain

It is significant that they were concerned about being surpassed not only in trade but also in artistic merit, which they associated with success in the marketplace—a concept that may seem naive today but one that is devoutly to be wished for.

As far as I can judge, French design was not surpassed—at least in textiles. French and British textile designers competed with each other in similar styles, and both were encouraged to reach for higher standards of excellence by the influential decorative-arts museums in Paris and London. Thereafter the competitive success of French vs. British textiles fluctuated with the tides of fashion so that little is to be gained by debating the relative artistic merits of the two.

For contemporary designers and students the important result of this competition is the textile collection itself. And that is not debatable. The best work of French textile designers—together with many examples from other cultures—has found a permanent place in the Musée des Arts Décoratifs.

Lack of Exhibit Space

Unfortunately, little of this rich heritage is currently

visible to the ordinary museum visitor. At this writing the Textile Department has no public galleries assigned to it, and all its impressive holdings are stored away in cabinets and glass-enclosed shelves that overflow the department's curatorial offices. Hopefully, this will change. I was told that a large public gallery on the first floor of the museum will eventually be devoted to textile exhibits. During my several visits to the museum, however, I found that the textile collection could be examined only with difficulty—though with the willing help of co-operative staff members.

I am sure that this condition will improve in the future. The authorities could not possibly allow so important a collection to remain in limbo for long. In the meantime an appointment must be made to explore the collection, and it is best to know which specific area you wish to examine. On this basis the material can usually be found without too much difficulty and will be opened for your inspection by knowledgeable staff members.

Survey of the Collection

Because of these problems the survey that follows is based on a far from adequate personal examination of the holdings. It is compiled largely from the inventory list especially prepared for me by Nadine Gasc and her associates—Mesdames Sfez, Viseux, and Schildg. For this difficult task I herewith express my gratitude.

The survey follows:

1. Coptic. About 300 fragments of tapestry weaving from Egypt, dating from the 5th to the 8th Century.

2. Woven Silks I. Over 6,000 pieces, dating from the 10th to the 20th Century. There are examples of many types—velvets, brocades, lampas, etc. The largest and most important group consists of 18th-Century French silks woven in Lyon and other centers. There is also good representaton of very early work from the Byzantine Empire, as well as examples of elaborate silk weaving from Persia, Turkey, England, Italy, Spain, Portugal, Germany, and Czarist Russia.

Modern French fabrics of the 20th Century form two special groups. The first covers fabrics dating from 1900–1960. The second group consists of annual donations of contemporary fabrics from French mills, beginning in 1960. There are thousands of samples in the latter group, and they are now in the process of being inventoried. They are not included in the count of 6,000 pieces.

3. Woven Silks II. About 2,000 pieces from China and Japan, woven in the 18th and 19th Centuries. These are often elaborately patterned textiles, sometimes in crisp geometric figures. The whole group is beautifully preserved and mounted on boards.

4. Painted Textiles. About 1,500 pieces. Chiefly work of the 18th and 19th Centuries from France, China, Japan, and the Indies.

5. Printed Textiles. More than 2,000 pieces, covering a long time span from the 10th Century to the present. The largest group is French work of the 18th and 19th Centuries, including many fine examples of Toiles de Jouy from the Oberkampf printworks. Other sources are Italy, Great Britain, India, the East Indies, Indonesia, Laos, Central Asia, Switzerland, Egypt, Persia, China, and Japan. The group also includes contemporary French prints from the year 1960 forward—now being inventoried and not included in the 2,000 figure.

6. Swatch Albums—Wovens. A vast collection of some 4,000 albums filled mainly with samples of woven silk and woolen fabrics. They cover the 18th and 19th Centuries. The work is predominantly French, but there are also many examples from Italy and Great Britain.

One British example has a special historic interest. It was assembled by Captain John Holker in 1750 (GG2-6752). It consists of 136 swatches of silks, cottons, linens, and blended fabrics, all made in Lancashire, England and chiefly in Manchester mills during the first half of the 18th Century.

Each of the 4,000 albums contains between 700 and 2,000 swatches—making a total of at least 5 million examples.

7. Swatch Albums—Prints. Another huge collection of about 2,500 albums, covering a period from the 18th to the early 20th Century. These are printed fabrics, mostly cotton, originating in France, Great Britain, and Germany. Among them are rare Oberkampf sample books for the years 1795–1805. Each of the 2,500 albums holds between 1,500 and 2,500 swatches—making a total of 4 to 6 million pieces.

8. Original Designs & Proofs. The museum owns some 1,500 volumes filled with thousands of original textile designs and printers' proofs on paper, showing designs in repeat. They date from the 18th to the 20th Century. The work is French and Italian.

9. Mises en Cartes. Another collection of designs on paper. There are 200 albums in the collection, each with

design layouts on graph paper, ready for production (mises en cartes). They come from France and Italy and date from the 18th and 19th Centuries. Each of the 200 albums holds between 50 and 100 designs—a total of over 15,000 pieces.

10. Livres de Remettage. This is a group of 250 weavers' record books, showing samples of fabric together with detailed notes on the method of construction (number of warp and weft yarns, etc.). They also come from France and Italy, 18th and 19th Centuries. Each album contains 50 to 100 samples—a total of perhaps 20,000 pieces.

11. Japanese Stencils. This is undoubtedly one of the world's largest collections of Japanese stencils. There are 3,000 pieces in the group, all 19th-Century work. Such stencils are owned by many museums but seldom in such large numbers. Since the art of stencil cutting was marvelously refined in Japan, these pieces represent a rich source of contemporary print design.

12. Embroideries. A major collection of about 10,000 pieces, dating from the 16th to the 20th Century. Again, the largest group is French. Other countries represented are Italy, Spain, Portugal, and adjacent areas in the Mediterranean basin, Poland, Rumania, Bulgaria, Austro-Hungary, and other areas in Central Europe. Included in the collection is an interesting group of about 50 "broderies en perles."

13. Lace. About 3,500 examples of work from the 17th to the 20th Century. All the important lacemaking centers of France are represented, together with good examples of lacemaking skill from Italy, Belgium, Holland, Germany, Great Britain, Ireland, and Spain.

14. Trimmings. About 15,000 samples of French trimming work (passementerie) for both home furnishings and costume. The collection covers examples of work from the 17th to the 20th Century and includes decorations for valances, bed covers, banners, and many types of apparel.

15. Costumes & Accessories. There are about 1,500 full costumes in the collection, and the emphasis is on French dress from the 16th to the 20th Century. All major periods and styles are represented. Also included are costumes from Central Europe, Yugoslavia, Spain, China, Japan, Syria, Morocco, Algeria, Tunisia, and some areas of Black Africa.

The accessories are numerous, but no count of them has yet been made. They include corsets, hose, gloves, shawls, footwear, coiffures, hats, purses, bags, parasols, and fans. All are of French origin.

16. Religious Ornaments. Ecclesiastical vestments and decorations number about 250 pieces, chiefly from France, Italy, and Spain. The work covers a time span from the 15th to the 19th Century.

17. Rugs. The rug and carpet collection is a most important one, numbering about 1,500 pieces and ranging from early work of the 16th Century to the present. It includes fine examples of rugmaking from France, Persia, several regions of the Near East, and the Far East.

18. Tapestries. The tapestry collection is one of the largest and most important in France—a country that abounds in tapestry collections. It covers a period from the 15th Century to contemporary times. The work is predominantly French, Belgian, and German. A large number of the French tapestries are exhibited in the public galleries of the museum.

The Decorative Arts Library

The library of the Musée des Arts Décoratifs has its own entrance at 109 rue de Rivoli. It is under the directon of Mme. Geneviève Picon, who is Chief Curator of the museum. In some measure Mme. Picon's title underlines the importance of this leading research facility, which specializes in books and documents on the decorative arts.

The library holdings were founded on the art scrapbooks of the collector Jules Maciet, which he began to assemble in 1870. It was opened as a free library at the turn of the century, and today it owns over 1 million prints, drawings, and photographs, as well as 80,000 volumes and 60,000 original designs—all in the decorative arts.

Among the rich resources is an incredibly varied collection of documentary design material for the textile designer—much of it arranged on open shelves in the long reading room and therefore easily accessible without the help of attendants. These design documents are pasted onto sheets and bound into large volumes, each 16 by 20 inches in size. They consist of engravings, photographs, and reproductions covering 493 separate subjects from worldwide sources. Among them are such diverse themes as animals, architecture, jewelry, ceramics, interior decor, mosaics, goldsmith work, plant forms, sculpture, vases, enamels, and textiles.

LEFT. The library on the ground floor of the Musée des Arts Décoratifs, Paris. Some of the large volumes with documentary design material are shown on the right. Over 470 volumes cover costume; over 150, textiles.

RIGHT. Point de Gaze lace collar, c. 1850, from the Musée d'Oze collection in Alençon (49.5.1). Similar lace collars and coifs in great numbers are held by the Musée des Arts et Traditions Populaires, Bois de Boulogne, Paris.

In the textile section there are currently 156 volumes, comprising the following categories: textiles (35 volumes), embroidery (34), lace (18), banners (5), draperies (5), rugs (7), tapestries (45), and religious vestments (7).

In addition a special alcove in the library contains open shelves with about 150 volumes of textile swatches and original textile designs—dating from the early 19th Century forward. These are kept accessible for the use of textile-design students.

There is also a big section of 472 volumes devoted to the international costume arts in 47 different categories, covering women's and men's dress, theatrical costumes, military uniforms, and all types of costume accessories.

The basement of the library houses the thousands of swatch volumes listed in the textile-department inventory.

During the period of my visits the basement storage sections of the library were undergoing extensive renovation. This is part of an overall program that includes the future establishment of a center for textile-design documentation. Plans call for a full catalog system listing textiles, swatch books, and design albums by categories or subjects. If and when this is achieved, the Musée des Arts Décoratifs will become one of the world's most important centers for the study of textiles.

Photographic Services

The museum maintains a photographic-service department, directed by Mme. Sonia Edard. It is equipped to make new photographs of all objects in the collection. It also has on file a substantial number of B/W negatives from which prints can be ordered. Many of these are of textiles, and sample prints can be examined in the offices of the Textile Department, where 11 albums of photographs are stored. A number of color slides, chiefly of 18th-Century French textiles, are also available.

PARIS

Musée National des Arts et Traditions Populaires
6, Route de Mahatma Gandhi   Metro: Sablons
Bois de Boulogne—Jardin d'Acclimatation
75116 Paris   TEL: 722-07-41

Curators: Mlle. Demoinet; Mme. Margerie

A well-known Parisian designer-weaver told me that she considered this museum the most stimulating research facility in Paris for textile design ideas. I can't quite agree, but I can understand her enthusiasm. The Museum of Popular Arts & Traditions collects and records examples of French folk culture from all regions of the country—with considerable panache.

It is a relatively new museum, opened in 1970. It occupies a handsome modern structure in the Bois de Boulogne, a pleasant five-minute walk from the Sablons Metro station and close to the children's zoo, with its amusement park and miniature railway (Jardin d'Acclimatation).

The public galleries of the museum fill two floors of the building. One of them is subterranean and has a distinctive display arrangement. It is laid out in "streets," or parallel corridors. There are nine such streets, lined on each side with exhibits behind plate glass so that they achieve the ambiance of an elegant shopping mall. The lighting is somewhat subdued, but in spite of this the visitor is given a rich and varied panorama of French country life.

Behind the show windows are hundreds of exhibits devoted to different aspects of traditional life in rural France—farm implements, tools, household interiors and furnishings, regional costumes for work and festivities.

There are only a handful of cottage-woven textiles on exhibit but about 200 garments—chiefly in Street No. 6. Here you can see smocks, vests, pants, jackets, capes, shawls, aprons, shirts, bags, and headdresses. These costume exhibits are the main attraction for textile designers, since they reveal many examples of cottage weaving, embroidery, and particularly lacework in coifs.

Reserve Collection

Displays in the public galleries represent only a fraction of the costume holdings owned by the museum—all held in reserve but available to researchers by appointment. This reserve collection holds about 6,000 pieces of costume and some 3,000 coifs with lace or embroidery. They come from all regions of rural France and present a fascinating picture of traditional country lifestyles, an invaluable record that preserves the customs and crafts of earlier times before they disappear forever.

Research Archives

And there are other facilities too—equally important to the researcher. On the sixth floor of the museum is the

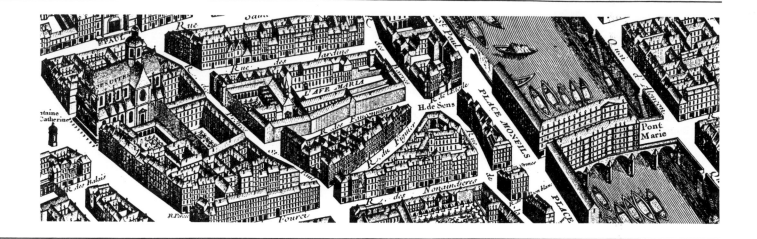

Service des Archives. This is a well-appointed facility (directed by Mme. Veyssière) that stores over 170,000 documents and photographs of regional life in France. Everything is efficiently cataloged and each catalog card carries a photograph of the piece described. For example, you can find photographs of villages and small towns all over France, as well as of the traditional craftwork and costumes found in both the public exhibits and the reserve collection.

Copies of all these photographs (as in other French national museums) are available from the *Service de Documentation Photographique de la Réunion des Musées Nationaux*, 89 Avenue Victor-Hugo, 75116 Paris. They must be ordered through the Service des Archives at the museum.

PARIS

Bibliothèque Forney
Hôtel des Archevêques de Sens
1, rue de Figuier   Metro: St. Paul
75004 Paris   TEL: 278-14-60

Mme. Jacqueline Viaux, Curator
Mme. Anne-Claude Lelieur, Asst.

For Art Deco and Art Nouveau designs the Forney Library is the best resource in Paris. And it owns many other original source materials and documents that will interest the textile designer.

The Forney Library is housed in a handsomely restored building that dates from the Middle Ages (1475–1519) and that was once the official Paris residence for the Archbishops of Sens. Though beautifully rebuilt, the exterior of the structure is still medieval in appearance, but its interior has been elegantly redesigned with modern, sophisticated lighting and library equipment. It is situated in the heart of the ancient Marais district, close to the Seine and the Ile St. Louis. An intriguing place even for a short visit and a most inviting facility for extended work.

No Obstacles to Research

The Forney was founded in 1886 by a Paris industrialist,

Aimé-Samuel Forney, with the specific aim of providing research facilities in design and technology for apprentices, artisans, students, teachers, and workers in all the decorative arts. It has continued to fill this need through the years and now more effectively than ever in the Hôtel de Sens, to which its holdings were transferred in 1961.

The library is operated by the Préfecture de Paris, and all its facilities are free. For example, residents of Paris may borrow up to 25 design documents at one time and may keep them for 15 days. Temporary visitors may also use the facilities with only minor restrictions.

This largesse is reflected in the easy accessibility of documents and in the helpfulness of staff. Everything in the library is clearly cataloged, and most of the material is arranged on open stacks so that it can be consulted at leisure and without pressure. A few of the rarer sample books are held in reserve stores, but they are quickly produced on demand.

The Fonds Iconographiques

Almost all the textile-design materials in the library are held on the fourth floor of the library (3e étage) in the section called Fonds Iconographiques. In all there are over 8,000 textile documents in various forms—swatch books, large samples in full repeat, pencil drawings, original watercolor designs on paper, and more than 2,000 examples of wallpaper design. A very rich and stimulating collection.

A few highlights will indicate the variety of source materials that a student or designer can expect to find here.

Art Deco. A section of open stacks in the fourth-floor reading room is given over to a substantial collection of original textile designs and reproductions. Filed by region, subject, or period and mounted on boards, the designs include work from the Far East as well as Europe, and they cover rugs as well as textiles. The biggest group is devoted to French textile design from the Middle Ages to the 20th Century, and it is here that one finds the important collection of original Art Deco designs in watercolor.

Most of these Art Deco designs fall within the period 1925–30 when abstract geometric patterns became a vogue following the Paris Exposition of Art Décoratifs (Art Deco) held in 1925. There are several hundred of these designs, and they form an evocative picture of a period when many painters of note began to experiment with textile designs—not always successfully but always with verve and imagination (see Color Section).

LEFT. Bird's-eye view of the Paris section in which the Bibliotheque Forney is situated, close to the Seine.

RIGHT. Though restored, the Hôtel de Sens, which houses the Forney library, still retains its medieval appearance. It was originally built between 1475 and 1519.

Art Nouveau. The influence of Art Nouveau on textile design is also reflected in the Forney collection—though not as extensively as the Art Deco material. The most important examples are the work of the Czech designer Alphonse Mucha (1860–1939). The Forney holds two famous Mucha designs—printed on both velvet and silk and in full repeat. They are *Femme Parmi les Fleurs* and *Femme à la Marguerite* (see Color Section). Both are superb examples of the Art Nouveau style and a high point of the Forney holdings.

Toiles de Jouy. This is a major collection of printed toiles from the Oberkampf works at Jouy as well as from other leading printing centers in France—one of the finest and most representative collections in the country. It was given to the Forney by Henri Clouzot, who was formerly the library's curator and the author of books that remain the most definitive works yet produced on French textile prints.

In all there are 19 large folios in the group—with hundreds of toile designs in full repeat. The work comes not only from Jouy but also from other major French printing centers such as Mulhouse, Nantes, Rouen, and Bordeaux. A detailed inventory of the collection is in preparation.

"Paisleys." The French term for these Indian (Kashmir) shawl designs is "Cachemire." French designers in this genre are claimed by many to have been superior to those of either England or Scotland—in both woven and printed versions. The Forney owns three large volumes of Cachemire print designs, and they provide superb evidence of the claim.

Lyon Silks. Five volumes of 19th-Century Jacquard silk fabrics from renowned weavers of Lyon; a sample book of silk ribbons by J. Leroudier, a Lyon manufacturer, covering the period 1840–1900; and four volumes of original designs (on paper) for Lyon silks.

The Potterlet Collection. One of the Forney's major assets is the collection of fabrics assembled by V. Potterlet. It consists of 16 volumes filled with swatches or drawings of 19th-Century French textiles, chiefly printed percales. One volume contains 684 swatches of prints made about 1850. A second volume has 779 swatches. A third volume holds designs and samples of machine-made lace from the 1850s. The other 13 volumes in the collection are equally rich in source material from the 19th Century.

The Moccasi Collection. Moccasi was an Italian collector who assembled examples of French, British, and Dutch textiles made during the 18th Century. One large volume holds the whole collection, but it is filled to capacity with hundreds of interesting swatches dated about 1760.

The Guerbette Collection. Several salesmen's sample books of 18th-Century French textiles issued by the house of Guerbette, textile dealers of Versailles.

Lace & Embroidery. Three large files filled with original French designs for lace and embroidery.

Wallpapers. Over 2,000 examples of French wallpaper design from the 19th and 20th Centuries.

The above represents no more than a sampling of the large and interesting Forney textile holdings. Also available to the researcher is a vast collection of some 250,000 reproductions on various aspects of the decorative arts. Everything in the collection can be photographed, and the library maintains its own extensive file of color slides, from which excellent copies can be ordered.

PARIS

Bibliothèque Nationale
58, rue de Richelieu   Metro: Bourse
75084 Paris Cédex 02   TEL: 266-62-62

Mlle. Th. Kleindienst, Secretary General
Mlle. Galliot, Chief Curator

The National Library of France is a somewhat forbidding place, but, if you have the patience to breach the barriers of bureaucracy, your reward will be a memorable experience.

For the Bibliothèque Nationale—to most people's surprise—owns a textile collection. Though not large, it is a distinguished collection and well worth the effort it takes to explore it. This is after all one of the great libraries of the world but might be bypassed by designers unaware of its textile holdings.

The bureaucratic barriers are not difficult to breach, merely tedious, not really different from those that obtain in other European libraries. Nor is it necessary to communicate with the officialdom in order to examine the textile collection. You enter the library, pass muster as a legitimate researcher, and sign up for a reader's card, which is good for two days.

Your objective is a section of the library known as Le Cabinet des Estampes on the second floor. (In an American

PARIS BIBLIOTHEQUE NATIONALE Continued

library or museum this might be known as the Print Department.) Once in the Cabinet des Estampes, you choose a numbered seat, consult a voluminous loose-leaf catalog for the holdings on Tissus, and fill out an order form for each volume or document that you wish to examine. An attendant will bring the document to your seat.

That is, if it can be found. In my case for some unexplained reason most of the documents that I wanted were unobtainable and I found myself completely frustrated until an intelligent young librarian suggested that I might wish to explore the stacks (*magazins*) where textile documents are stored—Section Lh on the second floor.

This is the approach I would recommend to all researchers. Once in Section Lh, everything I wanted to examine was at my fingertips. It is no more than a small alcove among miles of corridors and shelves, but it holds some of the most interesting textile material I have seen anywhere. In all, Section Lh holds over 100 large volumes. They are filled with thousands of textile swatches and textile designs on paper.

Following is a rundown of the most interesting documents.

1. Richelieu Collection (*Lh 45-45F*). This is a series of seven large volumes, each 13 by 18 inches, which contain exactly 4,818 samples of fabric. It was assembled between 1732 and 1737 by the Maréchal de Richelieu (not Cardinal Richelieu) and presents his year-by-year record of textiles bought for the royal households. There are silks, wools, worsteds, felts, and ribbons of every type fashionable in the period. The textiles are not only French but also English, Italian, Dutch, and Swiss. There are examples of clothing fabrics, table linens, drapery, upholstery, and ribbons. Some swatches are tiny; others, quite large. And each is accompanied by a fine calligraphic note describing the origin of the fabric, its use, and often its price. A remarkable record for textile historians with many ideas for designers.

Another large folio assembled by Richelieu (*Lh 40*) is devoted to textiles for fashionable clothing made between 1720 and 1735. It contains several hundred swatches of silks, velvets, and ribbons.

2. Tours Silks (*Lh 44-44d*). Five big volumes with hundreds of swatches, original drawings, and design tracings of silks made in Tours from 1720 to 1750. Tours, like Lyon, was a famous center of silk weaving (La Soierie Tourangelle)

but no large collection of its work is preserved in France today, so these five volumes represent one of the most important records still extant. Even the collection at the Musée des Beaux-Arts in Tours numbers only 420 pieces.

3. Royal Liveries (*Lh 23*). This is a large volume of swatches showing fabrics made in 1779 for the liveries of attendants in the royal household.

4. Shawl Designs (*Lh 129*). Four fat volumes of shawl designs (Cachemires) undated but probably 19th-Century work. French artists excelled in this type of "Paisley" design, and the work shown in these volumes is brilliant both in concept and execution. In all, the four volumes contain about 300 designs in full repeat, painted in watercolor and in a fine state of preservation. For me this was the outstanding treasure in the Cabinet des Estampes.

5. Indiennes (*Lh 54e*). Nine large volumes holding thousands of printed fabric swatches and hundreds of original designs on paper. All were produced by an unknown Mulhouse manufacturer between the years 1830 and 1880. They record the changing styles of "Indienne" print design during this fifty-year period.

6. Embroidery (*Lh 22*). A volume of original embroidery designs by Lafitte for uniforms of the royal household between 1815 and 1830.

7. Lace & Embroidery Pattern Books. A large number of early pattern books for lace and embroidery designs published in France, Italy, Germany, Flanders, and England. Several are dated in the year 1527, and other dates extend into the late 19th Century.

8. Design Ideas. A volume dated 1837 and titled *Musée du Dessinateur de Fabrique* (*Lh 53*). It is filled with fine pattern-work of the period.

9. Lyon Silks. *L'Art de Décorer les Tissus—1900* (*Lh 49a*) is a collection of designs and motifs taken from the important holdings of silks at the Musée Historique des Tissus in Lyon. It has excellent color plates, each of which contains reproductions of five or six swatches.

10. Original Textile Designs (*Lh 41*). This is an interesting volume dated 1730. It contains original designs for textiles in pencil and wash. Most of the patterns are well-executed florals.

These ten documents are the ones I found most interesting, but there are many others worthy of careful examination among the more than 100 large volumes stored in Section Lh of the Cabinet des Estampes.

RIGHT. Mousseline des Indes costume embroidered with sequins in the Directoire style. It was made in 1795. *Carnavalet—Musée du Costume, Paris.*

Chinese Textiles—2nd Century B.C.

Outside the Cabinet des Estampes the Chinese Section of the Bibliothèque Nationale holds a few interesting textiles. These are ten fragments of ancient silks made in China during the 2nd Century B.C. They were discovered by the Paul Pelliot expedition at Tuan-Huang, a stop on the ancient Silk Route at the edge of the Gobi Desert. These ten pieces are part of a larger collection from the same expedition. The remainder (93 pieces) are held by the Musée Guimet in Paris (See review under Guimet).

Photographs. The Service Photographique at the Bibliothèque Nationale supplies photographs (at modest prices) of all documents in the collections. Many of the most representative pieces in the Cabinet des Estampes have already been photographed by the Library's Photothèque. Black-and-white prints of these negatives can be examined in a series of folders stored in open shelves at the rear of the reading room in the Cabinet des Estampes. It is worth examining these photographs before exploring Section Lh in the stacks.

Catalog. A partial listing of the holdings in Section Lh is available from the librarians in the Cabinet des Estampes. It was prepared by Henri Bouchot and contains a rundown of the most important volumes in the section on pages 207–212. Photocopies of these pages are obtainable in the library.

PARIS

Carnavalet — Musée du Costume de la Ville de Paris
23, rue de Sévigné   Metro: St. Paul
75003 Paris   TEL: 272-21-13

Mlle. Madeleine Delpierre, Curator

(NOTE. The Musée du Costume formerly occupied its own building at 11 Avenue President-Wilson, but the building was closed for repairs, and at this writing the costume collection is stored in the annex of the Musée Carnavalet at the above address. This collection should not be confused with another Paris costume collection—the Centre d'Enseignement et de Documentation du Costume at 105, Blvd. Malesherbes.)

The Musée du Costume owns no flat textiles or swatches, but it has much to interest the textile designer and student. The collection consists of about 20,000 pieces. Some 4,500 of these are garments; the remainder are costume accessories. They cover a period from the mid-18th Century (1735) to modern times.

Mlle. Delpierre is most knowledgeable about the fabrics used in the garments under her care. For example, she showed me very interesting examples of warp prints, passementerie, silk stripings, cut velvets, amazingly intricate embroideries, sumptuous silks from Lyon and Tours, floating warp weaves, and many other types of complicated fabrics made before the advent of the Jacquard loom. I was particularly interested in her description of Point Rentré—a weaving technique that simulates embroidery. It was invented in 1735 by a Lyon textile manufacturer called Revel, and the example I was shown is the oldest piece in the costume collection.

The Musée du Costume has traditionally presented different facets of its collection in annual public exhibits—each with an accompanying catalog. They have included exhibitions of vests (1962–3), lace and embroidery (1964–5), and fashions of the Twenties (1970–1).

I should add that at this writing the collection can be examined only by appointment and even then with great difficulty because of the cramped and dusty quarters in which it is stored. It is to be hoped that the City of Paris will soon find an adequate home in which to exhibit and make accessible this important record of its fashion history.

PARIS

Centre d'Enseignement et de Documentation du Costume (Union Française des Arts du Costume)
105, Boulevard Malesherbes   Metro: Villiers
75008 Paris   TEL: 387-19-26

Mlle. Yvonne Deslandres, Director
Mlle. Catherine Bonnin, Public Relations

(NOTE. The Centre should not be confused with the Musée du Costume now located in the Carnavalet annex.)

This is one of the world's richest collections of historic

PARIS CENTRE DU COSTUME Continued

French costume, modern Paris haute couture, and fashion-fabric swatches—on a par with such facilities as the Costume Institute and the F.I.T. Design Lab in N.Y. or the Gallery of English Costume in Manchester. It is operated by the Union Française des Arts du Costume, which was founded in 1948 and which established the Centre in 1961, first at 79 Ave. de la République and now at the above address.

Having said this, it seems hardly credible that I must describe in some detail how a visitor reaches the place, for it is difficult to find—in itself a strange anomaly in the fashion capital of the world.

You must, of course, telephone in advance to announce your visit. When you reach 105, Boulevard Malesherbes, you will find a large archway leading to an undistinguished dead-end mews. It is filled with parked cars, delivery trucks, and the ground-floor offices of several small businesses. You walk to the back of the mews, which is blocked by a high iron fence. In the fence is a locked iron door painted orange (a fashion color?) and an inconspicuous sign to tell you that this is the entrance to the Centre. You are instructed to ring a bell, and your ring is answered by a disembodied voice issuing from a loudspeaker. You are asked to identify yourself, and, if acceptable, the door will be opened by a remote-control buzzer. The first hurdle has been surmounted. You now cross an alley and mount a steep wooden staircase to the top floor.

I recommend a slow approach, for it is a stiff climb. You will be ascending the backstairs entrance to the elegant Camondo mansion, whose front door is around the corner at 63, rue de Monceau (Musée Nissim de Camondo). And when you reach the top of the stairs, you will find yourself in the attic servant quarters of the Count de Camondo's distinguished townhouse, with its luxurious Louis XVI decor. (It is now a gem of a small museum devoted to 18th-Century art and furnishings.) The Centre's quarters are on loan from the Union Centrale des Arts Décoratifs, which controls the Camondo Museum as well as the Musée des Arts Décoratifs at the Louvre Palace.

In short, reaching the Center is not easy, but it is well worth the effort. The attic rooms are crammed to overflowing with a fabulous collection whose highlights include the following:

1. About 5,000 full fashion ensembles and some 30,000 fashion accessories—all French and dating from the 18th Century to the current year. They include representative garments or drawings from all the important Paris couture houses as well as regional peasant costumes from many parts of France.

2. A collection of large folios that contains close to 60,000 swatches of haute-couture fabrics from leading French textile houses. More on this later.

3. 25,000 original designs for costumes and hats from famous couture houses in Paris. Also 8,000 fashion plates.

4. Close to 75,000 photographs of fashions dating from 1860–1970.

5. Over 2,000 retail-store catalogs of fashions dating from the 18th Century forward.

6. About 5,500 photographic negatives recording the history of costume, many with details of the fabrics used.

7. Some 6,000 fashion periodicals from 1825 to the present, plus about 50 current subscriptions to contemporary fashion journals. Also most of the important published works, both ancient and modern, on the subject of costume.

8. A unique index-card "dictionary" of definitions for both costume and textile terms. It is still in process, and at this writing it contains 18,000 entries. The "dictionary" is being prepared by Mme. Boucher, wife of François Boucher, who was a founder of the Centre. He is author of the authoritative and beautifully illustrated work on costume titled *20,000 Years of Fashion* (Harry N. Abrams, N.Y.).

The Swatch Collection

For textile designers the most rewarding facet of the Centre collection is the large range of textile swatches stored in its library study room. Among the nearly 60,000 pieces on file here there are apparel fabrics going back as far as the 18th Century (800 swatches) and forward to the current season. Perhaps the richest and most stimulating group comes from the famous fabric house of Rodier, whose complete production for the years 1835–1920 is represented here (35,000 swatches).

Another important group consists of 800 embroidery designs from the house of Bataille. There is also a collection of apparel wools from the house of Meyer and a collection of lingerie that is generally considered to be the most important of its kind in the world. And this textile collection is constantly expanding, with examples of each year's production collected by the Chambre Syndicale des Tissus

RIGHT. One of the six panels in the tapestry group known as *La Dame à la Licorne*. It is beautifully housed in a large circular gallery at the top of the Cluny Museum. It was woven at the end of the 15th Century and is the highpoint of the Cluny's medieval textile collection.

and the Syndicat Français des Textiles Artificiels et Synthetiques.

With a collection of such richness and diversity it is to be hoped that the Centre will soon find a more accessible home and one more worthy of its holdings.

Publication. Some of the richness and vitality of resources at the Centre is revealed in a recent book by Yvonne Deslandres, its director. It is *Le Costume, Image de l'Homme*, published by Albine Michel.

PARIS

Musée de Cluny

(Musée des Thermes et de l'Hôtel de Cluny)
6, Place Paul-Painlevé   Metro: Odéon or St. Michel
75005 Paris Cédex   TEL: 325-62-00

Mlle. A. Lefébure, Curator
Mlle. Thibaudat, Assistant

The Cluny is a gem of a museum devoted to arts and crafts of the Middle Ages—5th to 15th Century. Its home is a Late Gothic mansion built at the end of the 15th Century for the Abbots of Cluny in Bourgogne. This is the Hôtel de Cluny, which rests on the site of an ancient Roman palace (2–3rd Century) whose partly ruined baths (Thermes de Lutèce) form the western wing of the museum. Not a bombed-out ruin, as it may appear to the tourist, but a piece of living French history in the center of a busy student precinct where the Blvd. St. Germain crosses the Blvd. St. Michel.

It is also a perfect setting for the small but renowned collection of medieval textiles and tapestries that the Cluny owns and exhibits. The majority of them are concentrated in two galleries—Room III and Room XI. Room III is referred to as La Salle des Tissus. Room XI is the big circular gallery built especially for the six magnificent panels of *The Lady with the Unicorn* tapestries (*La Dame à la Licorne*).

The following brief notes are therefore devoted to the contents of these two galleries.

La Salle des Tissus

This is a small gallery with permanent exhibits of some 200 medieval textiles—many of them fragments. The lighting is poor (though scheduled for improvement), but the display arrangements are good. Everything is behind glass, but this is something of an asset, since it allows the visitor to examine the patternwork quietly and without interference from attendants. Some displays are mounted on the walls, but the majority are shown in the wide, shallow drawers of large file cases. Visitors are free to open the drawers and examine the contents laid out under glass.

For example, case No. 200 holds fragments of textiles dating from the 7th to the 15th Century and originating in Egypt (Sassanian), Persia, Italy, Sicily, and Spain.

Elsewhere in the display cases are many Coptic fragments, examples of Byzantine, Flemish, and early German weaving, as well as additional pieces of Egyptian, Persian, Byzantine, Italian, and Spanish textile art. Among them are a number of richly embroidered ecclesiastical vestments.

A summary of the holdings displayed in La Salle des Tissus shows the following breakdown:

Coptic Textiles, 4–11th Century—about 50 pieces
Other Egyptian Textiles, 7–12th Century—about 60
Byzantine Textiles, 4–11th Century—about 10
Italian & Sicilian Textiles, 14–15th Century—about 40
German Textiles—about 15
Spanish Textiles, 12–15th Century—about 10

This does not seem a large number for so renowned a textile collection, but the rarity of the pieces and the interest of the patternwork more than make up for the modest size.

Tapestries—*La Dame à la Licorne*

The Cluny owns about 40 medieval tapestries, and a number of them are displayed on the walls of the galleries—particularly in Galleries III and IV. They give us an evocative picture of medieval life, but for me the chief glory of the Cluny collection has long been the set of six millefleurs tapestries known as *La Dame à la Licorne*, woven at the end of the 15th Century and probably in France.

Many designers have seen photographs of these six large panels—the smallest over 10 feet square. Many may also have seen the originals when they were on loan in the vast Masterpieces of Tapestry exhibit at the Metropolitan Museum of Art in New York (1974). But to see them in all their roseate splendor, one must climb to the top of the

Cluny and enter the skylit rotunda that was especially designed to do them justice.

In this serene environment filled with natural light, the panels sing from the walls. I believe that much early tapestry work is seldom a stimulating resource for contemporary textile design, but *La Dame à la Licorne* is a brilliant exception to this possibly arbitrary judgment. It is not so much that the millefleurs backgrounds suggest textile pattern ideas—which they do. Rather it is the total ambiance of the graceful figures, the elegant composition, and the soft, roseate colors that can induce in the designer a mood and an attitude stimulating to inspired design. An hour spent in this lovely setting among these great works of art can become a memorable experience for every textile designer.

The Reserve Collection

Besides the textiles described above, the Cluny holds another collection of textiles that is larger than the medieval group on exhibit in the galleries. It numbers about 850 pieces, chiefly made in the 16th Century. This whole collection is held in reserve, however, and is not at this writing available to researchers. I am informed that the major part of the reserve collection will be transferred within a few years to a new home now being prepared for it. This will be the Museum of the Renaissance and will be established in the Chateau d'Ecouen, 21 km. north of Paris.

Photographs. Most of the textiles and tapestries on exhibit at the Cluny have been photographed in black-and-white. Prints are on file in the curator's office at the museum, where they can be examined. Copies can be ordered from the *Service de Documentation Photographique de la Réunion des Musées Nationaux*, 89 Avenue Victor-Hugo, 75116 Paris.

PARIS

Musée Guimet

6, Place d'Iéna   Metro: Iéna
75116 Paris   TEL: 723-61-65

Mlle. Jeannine Auboyer, Chief Curator
Mlle. M. M. Deneck, Curator

The Guimet Museum, holds one of the world's richest collections of Asiatic art—but few textiles. This, in spite of the interesting fact that the museum's first home (in 1879) was in the textile city of Lyon. Its founder, Emile Etienne Guimet (1836–1918), was a Lyon industrialist who operated a color-pigment factory that produced the synthetic ultramarine dye invented by his chemist father, Jean-Baptiste Guimet, in 1828.

However, though the textile collection is small (less than 150 pieces in all), it has some very rare holdings. It contains one of the few records outside China that shows us the kind of silk textiles transported along the ancient 6,000-mile Silk Route from China to the Mediterranean.

There are exactly 93 ancient Chinese textile fragments in the collection. Many have decorative patternwork, and some can be dated as early as the Han Dynasty (206 B.C. to 220 A.D.). They were discovered in graves at Tuan-huang by the Paul Pelliot expedition, together with 10 additional fragments now held by the Bibliothèque Nationale in Paris. Tuan-huang is in the province of Kansu. It was an oasis on the edge of the Gobi Desert and a communications center along the Silk Route. The fabrics discovered there are believed to be representative examples of the commercial Chinese silks that were so important a commodity in the ancient merchant caravans—fabrics as costly and as highly prized in those times as gold and fine jewels.

Many of the fragments in the collection are in a poor state of preservation, but the patternwork is quite visible and the constructions have been carefully analyzed. They have become the subject of a technical treatise by Krishna Riboud and Gabriel Vial, Secretary of CIETA in Lyon. The work is titled *Tissus de Touen-houang Conservés au Musée Guimet et à la Bibliothèque Nationale*. It was published in 1970 by L'Académie des Inscriptions et Belles-Lettres of Paris and is profusely illustrated with photographs and construction charts of these ancient fabrics.

* * *

Other Guimet Textiles. Aside from this rare Chinese collection the Guimet holds a few examples of 19th-Century Asiatic textile art. These include Gujarat and Bengal saris from India, a Champa embroidery from Tibet, painted textiles from Nepal (one dated 1488), and a fine collection of temple banners from both Tibet and Nepal.

LEFT. The two wings of the Palais de Chaillot. In the background the Eiffel Tower can be seen behind the statue. The Musée de l'Homme is housed in the wing on the right.

RIGHT. Rear view of the Musée de l'Homme with its curved wing. The gardens roll downhill to the Seine.

PARIS

Musée de l'Homme

(Muséum National d'Histoire Naturelle)
Palais de Chaillot   Métro: Trocadéro
75116 Paris   TEL: 727-57-78

Prof. Jean Guiart, Dir., Ethnological Section
Mme. Solange Thierry, Asst. Director

The Musée de l'Homme has many things to recommend it—among them a truly spectacular view from the hilltop terrace of the Palais de Chaillot. From here you look straight at the looming colossus of the Eiffel Tower straddling the great plain of the Champ de Mars below.

The collection of ethnographic textiles and costumes is large, varied, and among the most exciting I know for textile designers. It holds some 17,000 pieces, efficiently distributed among six departments—each with its own knowledgeable curator and assistants, as well as separate storage facilities.

And the collections are all choice, selected with an educated taste and with a rich knowledge of the cultures they represent, for the Musée de l'Homme is one of the world's leading anthropological research institutions.

Everything Available for Study

Equally if not more important is the fact that all pieces in the collections are accessible. I emphasize this accessibility, since it is often not true of ethnographic collections elsewhere—a situation that generally discourages designers and students. It is therefore a pleasure to find that the textile collections at the Musée de l'Homme are clearly cataloged, that the storage facilities are easy to reach, and that the curatorial staff knows exactly where to find what the visitor wants to examine.

The Photothèque

Add to this that the Musée de l'Homme has a photographic department (Photothèque) that is a joy to explore. It is one of the most extensive and well-organized departments of this kind in the whole museum field and full of revelatory discoveries for the designer.

The Photothèque holds some 100,000 negatives, about 300,000 black-and-white prints, 20,000 color transparencies

on glass, and about 7,000 35-mm. slides and Ektachromes. It is especially strong in late 19th-Century photographs, including objects owned by the museum as well as comparable material recorded by anthropologists in the field. Among this vast range of documentary material are thousands of textile-costume photographs.

This whole photographic collection is clearly cataloged by country and subject. Fine-quality copies of both black-and-white prints and color transparencies are made in the museum's own photographic labs and can be ordered through the efficient Mme. Patisson, who directs the work of the Photothèque. Her interest and helpfulness go far beyond the bounds of duty, and she speaks English, as do several of the curators at the museum.

The Library

On its fourth floor the Musée de l'Homme also has an important anthropological library, with over 180,000 volumes and about 3,500 periodicals. Its two reading rooms offer the researcher fine facilities, with about 15,000 volumes on open shelves in addition to complete sets of about 100 professional journals. The library is under the direction of M. Bayle.

The Textile Collections

The composite collections of some 17,000 textiles and costumes at the Musée de l'Homme are all held by the Ethnographic Department, Prof. Jean Guiart, Director. They are distributed among six separate departments, whose curators and approximate holdings follow:

Europe. Mme. Monique Roussel de Fontanès, Curator. This department holds the largest textile-costume collection in the museum. It contains over 7,000 pieces.

Asia. Mme. Solange Thierry, Curator; Bernard Dupaigne, Asst. Mme. Thierry is also Asst. Director of the Musée de l'Homme and is most helpful in all matters related to research. M. Dupaigne is a specialist on Afghanistan and is codirector of a 22-minute color film (1975) on the village craft of ikat in that region. The Asia Department holds the second largest textile-costume collection at the museum—about 5,500 pieces.

White Africa. Mme. Champault, Curator; Mlle. de Langle, Asst. Approximately 2,000 pieces.

Black Africa. Mme. N'Diaye, Curator. About 1,000 pieces.

America. Mme. Simoni, Curator; Mme. Fardoulec, Asst. About 1,200 pieces.

LEFT. Detail of a Mohammedan woman's embroidered robe from Israel. *Musée de l'Homme—67.42.7 (C.67.1510.493).*

RIGHT. Detail of a woman's legging in knitted wool from Greece. *Musée de l'Homme—57.51.30 (E.62.1030.493).*

FAR RIGHT. Embroidered border of an apron from Hungary, 64 cm. wide. *Musée de l'Homme—37.64.155 (C.68.72.493).*

PARIS MUSEE DE L'HOMME Continued

Oceania. Mlle. Girard, Mlle. Bataille, Curators. A small collection of about 300 pieces.

Following is a description of the more important holdings in each of these six departments.

European Textiles & Costumes

The textile-costume holdings from the European continent, as already noted, make up the largest single unit of the six groups—close to 7,000 pieces. They consist of 19–20th-Century peasant costumes and flat fabrics—woven, printed, or embroidered. They represent the folk cultures of some 30 distinct European cultures, but about one-third of the total comes from Yugoslavia—over 2,200 pieces.

In broad outline the European group shows the following breakdown:

Complete Costumes—about 300 pieces.
Separate Garments—about 2,000 pieces.
Headdresses, Hats, etc.—about 1,250 pieces.
Rugs & Household Textiles—about 700 pieces.
Samples of Weaving & Embroidery—about 2,500 pieces.

In addition to the major holdings from Yugoslavia there are fairly substantial holdings of 200–500 pieces from the following eight countries: Albania (226), Bulgaria (396), Czechoslovakia (434), Estonia (249), Greece and the Greek Islands (289), Hungary (328), Portugal (361), and Rumania (505).

The remaining examples, in smaller but representative groups, come from the following countries:

Austria, Balkans, Belgium, Cyprus, Denmark, Finland, France, Germany, Holland, Iceland, Ireland, Italy, Lithuania, Luxembourg, Malta, Norway, Poland, Spain, Sweden, Switzerland, Turkey, and the U.S.S.R. (Russia, Ukraine, Byelorussia, Moldavia, Karelia, Crimea).

The Yugoslavian Collection. This group of over 2,200 textiles and costumes deserves special attention. It is considered one of the largest and finest collections of such materials outside Yugoslavia. It covers all types of peasant costumes for men, women, and children as well as a wide range of peasant household textiles. But from a designer's point of view perhaps the most interesting facet of the collection is a large group of over 300 belts and sashes,

chiefly from the Serbian section of the country. Many of them are narrow women's marriage belts, closely and intricately woven in sharply etched geometric patternings. They often resemble the traditional woven belts found in Guatemala but are quite distinctive in their own right, surprisingly modern in their design concepts, and contain a wealth of good design ideas for contemporary textiles.

I should add that the whole collection in the European Department is very well organized for research and all textile swatches are neatly mounted on boards for easy reference. Altogether a most rewarding source of textile-design inspiration.

The Asian Collections

The Asian Department at the Musée de l'Homme owns representative textiles and costumes from more than a dozen different regions, and its total holdings number about 5,500 pieces. A breakdown of the major units follows:

Vietnam, North & South	1,040
India	900
Afghanistan & U.S.S.R.	625
China & Burma	570
Turkey (including rugs)	500
Iran & Iraq	425
Laos, Cambodia, & Thailand	360
Japan	115
Pakistan	105
Ceylon	15

This large and diverse collection is stored in some thirty steel double cabinets, 8 feet high, and arranged along an interior corridor that follows the curve of the Palais de Chaillot. Most pieces are packed in transparent plastic covers, and every piece is easily accessible. Following are a few highlights from this wide-ranging group:

● A superb collection of about 25 silk-ikat robes from Bukhara (U.S.S.R.) They were made in the late 19th and early 20th Centuries and reveal the traditional dramatic ikat patternings of Central Asia (*See Color Section*).

● From the same region comes a series of closely covered embroideries, tie-dye, and plangi fabrics.

● Ikats from Afghanistan, including some in patchwork.

● Rich examples of Turkish embroidery.

● Embroidered dowry garments from Pakistan.

- Indian textiles in several decorative techniques—painted-and-dyed, tie-dyed, and embroidered. The embroidery group includes pieces of Naga tribal art.

- Card weaving from Bangladesh.

- Japanese printing stencils—a fine collection dating from the early 19th Century.

- A large and unique group of embroideries from the Man people of North Vietnam. They consist of red and white cross-stitched designs on a dark navy ground.

These represent only a few of the many groups that suggest themselves as excellent sources for contemporary textile design. Several days would be required to explore the many facets of this rich collection.

White Africa—Textile Arts

The 2,000 or so pieces in the White African textile collection represent the textile arts of some 16 countries. Several were former French colonies, which may account in part for the richness of the selections. The countries with the best representation are: Algeria, Tunisia, Morocco, Mauritania, Senegal, Mali, Nigeria, Libya, Egypt, Saudi Arabia, Yemen, Syria, Jordan, Israel, and Iraq.

Most of the pieces are costumes, often with intricate embroidery in the tradition of the Arab and Berber tribes. The Palestinian embroidery is especially noteworthy, as are the woven Arab caftans. The work generally dates from the end of the 19th Century or early 20th Century.

Black Africa—Textile Arts

There are approximately 1,000 examples of textile craft in this department, originating chiefly in West and Central Africa. There are complete costume ensembles from different regions, a large number of women's robes (boubu), belts, sashes, and headgear. Most of the work is woven, and possibly the best representation comes from the Mandingo people of Mali. There are also good examples of traditional textile craft from the north Ivory Coast, Volta, and Senegal, as well as some narrow weavings of silk Kente cloth from the Ashanti of Ghana. Resist prints in the collection come from Mali and the Cameroons.

American Textile Arts

Though this collection is modest in size—about 1,200 pieces—it holds a remarkably wide range of textiles from many different cultures covering North, Central, and South America. The holdings are divided into two sections: (1) Archaeological and (2) Ethnographic.

Archaeological. The textile examples in this division are chiefly Peruvian and extend from the 3rd Century B.C. to the Inca civilization of the 16th Century. There are approximately 400 pieces in the group, with both woven and painted examples reflecting the cultures of Paracas, Chimu, Nazca, and the Central Coast.

Ethnographic. This is a larger group of about 750 pieces dating mainly from the 18th to the 20th Century. Following is a breakdown of the regions covered and the approximate number of pieces from each region: Guatemala (200), Mexico (150+), Bolivia (200+), Peru (30), Panama (10), and North American Indian (100). There is also token representation from Chile, Ecuador, Honduras, Costa Rica, and the Antilles.

Among these groupings I would like to call special attention to an unusual collection of Quechua Indian weavings from the Charazani region of Bolivia. They were acquired by a Musée de l'Homme expedition in 1964. They are narrow striped weavings of a remarkable aesthetic quality—shawls, sashes, belts, bags, ponchos, skirts. The design motifs are symbolic and take the forms of highly stylized birds, beasts, human figures, and geometric motifs—all intricately and harmoniously arranged within the confines of the narrow vertical stripes. The design aesthetic is quite sophisticated, and the whole collection is an unusually rich source for textile design themes.

The American Indian material is also worthy of note. Though it is not large, some of the pieces are early, dating from the 16th and 17th Centuries. There are good examples of quill embroidery, featherwork, and some exceptional painted skins from the Labrador Indians.

Textile Arts of Oceania

The regions covered by the textile holdings in this department are Indonesia, Melanesia, and Polynesia. It is a small collection—about 300 pieces in all. The largest unit consists of about 200 pieces of decorated tapa cloth from Samoa, Hawaii, Tahiti, the Solomon Islands, the Celebes, and New Guinea. There are also smaller groups of Indonesian fabrics and woven Tenaka border designs from New Zealand.

Perhaps the most outstanding unit in the Oceanic holdings is a group of woven-cotton ikats from the Indonesian

LEFT. Salle Copte #1 at the Louvre. It exhibits early Coptic textiles dating through the 5th Century. The archway leads to Salle Copte #2, which shows later pieces.

RIGHT. Salle Copte #2 at the Louvre. Coptic textiles of the 6–7th Century are displayed here. There are three galleries devoted to Coptic textiles, and they show about 80 of the best pieces in the collection—all well lighted.

PARIS MUSEE DE L'HOMME Continued

island of Sumba. Though there are only ten pieces in the unit, they are all exceptionally fine examples of the genre and reflect the three dominant styles of design that have given this little island so large a position among the world's textile cultures.

Gallery Exhibits

From each of the six departments outlined above choice and representative examples of textile art are on display in the two long public galleries of the Musée de l'Homme. As with most museums, the major textile holdings are held in reserve, but there are many fine pieces on exhibit behind glass—enough to indicate the richness of the whole collection and to stimulate the designer to further research. I was particularly interested in the following displays as sources for contemporary textile design:

1. *From Niger (Djerma People).* Great quilted covers for horse and rider, used as armor by the Sultan's horseguards. The fitted covers are constructed of colored-fabric triangles in a dramatic arrangement of blacks, reds, tans, whites, and yellows. Horse and man are covered head to foot.

2. *From the Congo (Bushongo).* Raffia-pile cloths in geometric patternings.

3. *From Madagascar (Malagasy).* Several examples of the Lamba—an oblong woven band of wild silk with ikat decorations.

4. *From the Levant.* A Bedouin saddlebag in subtle earth-tone colorings.

5. *From Algeria.* A splendid woven palanquin for a noble-woman, elaborately decorated with cowrie shells.

6. *From Mesopotamia.* A Baghdad rug in offbeat "funky" colors.

7. *From Bulgaria.* A superb example of folk embroidery in a marriage apron. (Case 229)

8. *From Japan.* An Ainu robe woven with elm-bark fibers. (Case 280)

9. *From Central Asia.* An embroidered Kirghiz robe. (Case 298)

10. *From Iran (Munisk).* An exceptionally fine example of a Turkman ikat robe (62.12.5).

11. *From Polynesia.* A stimulating display of patterned tapa cloths.

Publications

The Musée de l'Homme publishes *Objets et Mondes*—a quarterly journal devoted to ethnological research conducted under museum auspices. It frequently prints detailed and illustrated studies of textile arts in different parts of the world. Among such studies the following will be of special interest to textile designers:

1. "Tissus Décorés de l'Ile de Sumba." By Monni Adams. A fairly comprehensive survey of the styles and techniques used in Sumba ikats. 12 photographs. Vol. VI, No. 1, 1966.

2. "Lamak et Tissus Sacrés de Bali." By Christian Pelras. A discussion (with illustrations) of the designs and techniques used in making sacred temple banners and hangings in Bali. Vol. VII, No. 4, Winter 1967.

3. "Textiles Boliviens—Region de Charazani." By Louis Girault. This is a 165-page catalog devoted to the remarkable striped weavings mentioned earlier in this report. It is profusely illustrated with 84 clear photographs and precise graphic drawings, giving a detailed picture of the weavings and the stylized symbolic motifs found in these Bolivian textiles. Supplement to Vol. IX, No. 4, 1969.

4. "Un Artisan d'Afghanistan." By Bernard Dupaigne. The life and works of a master silk weaver and printer in rural Afghanistan. Illustrated. Vol. XIV, No. 3, 1974.

16-mm. Films

The Musée de l'Homme issues a continuing series of 16-mm. color films on many of the subjects published in *Objets et Mondes*. Among films currently available the following should be of interest to textile designers and students:

1. *Ikats d'Afghanistan* (1975). A 22-minute color film co-produced by Annie Zorz and Bernard Dupaigne. It shows and explains all the operations of silk-ikat production in an Afghanistan village.

2. *Un Village Turkmène* (1974). A 26-minute color film by the same team showing life in a northern Afghanistan village that specializes in silk weaving.

3. *La Fabrication d'un Feutre en Afghanistan* (1974). A 12-minute color film by the same team on felt making in a northern Afghanistan village.

Slide Kits. The Ethnology Department at the Musée de l'Homme recently launched a series of color-slide kits on various aspects of its collections. Plans are underway to expand this series with special kits on ethnological textiles.

PARIS

Musée du Louvre

Bureau de la Conservation
32 Quai du Louvre (Pont des Arts)   Metro: Louvre
75041 Paris Cédex 01   TEL: 260-39-26

Pierre du Bourguet, S. J., Curator, Egyptian
Antiquities

The Louvre has no textile department as such, but its
Department of Egyptian Antiquities holds a collection of
Coptic textiles that is probably the largest and most important in the world. For the student of textile design
this is without doubt the Louvre's major attraction.

Equally relevant is the fact that the Conservateur en Chef
of this collection is Père du Bourguet, a Jesuit priest who
is recognized as the world's leading authority on Coptic
textiles. A warm and sympathetic man, Père du Bourguet
passed two years of his youth as a student at Oxford, and he
speaks and writes English with ease. It was a rare privilege
for me to be guided by him through the Louvre's renowned
Coptic holdings and to recognize the authority with which
he explains this fascinating area in early textile history.

He believes that the Copts were expert weavers from at
least the 2nd Century B.C., for they were Egyptians before
they became Christians. Since they continued to produce
their distinctive decorative fabrics until the 12th Century
A.D., he speaks of their work as the only consistent evidence
that we now possess of ancient decorative-textile art as it
developed through the centuries.

Père du Bourguet has written a definitive study of Coptic
textiles (see full title under Publications). It is Volume
I of a projected two-volume catalog detailing the contents
of the Louvre's Coptic collection. But it is far more than
the usual catalog. It is a fat volume, a comprehensive
treatise that provides technical information, weaving
diagrams, and a careful dating of Coptic design periods.
It is profusely illustrated with black-and-white photographs
of pieces in the Louvre collection. In effect, a museum
without walls. Volume II of the work has been completed
but not yet published at this writing.

Size & Range of the Collection

The Louvre holds over 3,000 examples of Coptic textile
art, including some painted pieces. They cover a time span
from the 3rd to the 12th Century. The majority of the
pieces are either small or in fragmentary condition, but
at least 100 examples are of large dimension and among
the best-known pieces in the world.

Moreover, some 1,500 pieces—about half the collection—
came to the Louvre directly from the archaeological excavations in which they were found. Their provenance
and dating is therefore accurately known, which has
enabled Père du Bourguet to develop a complete panorama
of Coptic styles and design motifs as they evolved over
more than ten centuries.

According to his estimate the Louvre collection represents
about one-tenth of the 35,000 Coptic pieces known to be
held by museums throughout the world—many of which he
has examined personally.

La Salle Copte

The bulk of the Louvre's Coptic textiles are held in reserve, stored in cabinets that line a corridor of the Bureau
de la Conservation near Père du Bourguet's office. This
makes them somewhat difficult to examine, though an
appointment can be made to do so by qualified researchers.

About 80 of the most important pieces in the collection
are on permanent exhibit (behind glass) in three of the
galleries devoted to Egyptian Antiquities—La Salle Copte,
first floor, near the Venus de Milo. Here they are intelligently displayed close to sculpture and ceramics from the
same periods of Egyptian History. These 80 pieces cover
the full range of the Louvre's holdings and represent the
major styles and motifs in Coptic textiles from the 3rd to
the 12th Century.

In themselves—and without reference to the reserve
collection—these exhibits form the most comprehensive
and illuminating presentation of Coptic textile art I have
yet seen in any museum. Each example has been lovingly
preserved, restored, and mounted to best advantage. In
many cases the colors seem as clear and fresh as they must
have appeared when they first came off the loom.

Best of all, the exhibits are remarkably well lit. Père du
Bourguet differs from many textile curators in his belief
that rare and ancient fabrics can be judiciously exposed to
electric light without fear of fading or deterioration. At
the time of my visit the Coptic displays had been exposed
to electric light for about two years and I could detect no
sign of damage. The glass-enclosed panels are positioned

PARIS LOUVRE Continued

away from direct sunlight, and those pieces nearest the overhead electric light source are titled slightly forward to avoid direct light—but that is all.

Among the 80 or so examples on exhibit in the three galleries of La Salle Copte the following made the strongest impression on me:

1. A large panel, painted with stencils, showing scenes from the Dionysus myth. Antinöe, 3rd Century.

2. A fragment from a green tapestry-woven panel showing beautifully defined swimming fish. Dated 2-3rd Century. This is a section from a large panel (or a similar one) owned by the Musée Historique des Tissus in Lyon (see Color Section).

3. A child's shirt with intricate tapestry decorations in purple wool. 5–7th Century.

4. *Chale de Sabine.* A large reconstructed shawl or hanging on a muted red ground. Antinöe, 6th Century.

5. A large glass-enclosed wall panel with 32 separate pieces effectively grouped on a green plush background. In the center Père du Bourguet has sensitively placed a small 5th-Century wooden sculpture of the Virgin Mary spinning. The 32 pieces reveal an interesting variety of styles in Coptic tapestry decoration—from flower motifs and portrait heads to a beautifully articulated crowing cock about 16 inches high, whose design and execution have an amazing 20th-Century quality.

6. *Triumph of the Cross.* A large panel in raised loop weaving, with several charmingly executed themes. Among them are Jonah being swallowed by the whale and the tree in the Garden of Eden.

Other Textiles at the Louvre

In addition to Coptic textiles the Louvre owns a large collection of tapestries dating from the Middle Ages to the 18th Century, a few fine examples of Islamic silks, and decorative French draperies and wall coverings displayed in the Decorative Arts Department galleries around the Cour Carée on the second floor.

Publication. *Catalogue des Etoffes Coptes I. Musée National du Louvre.* By P. du Bourguet. Paris, Affaires Culturelles, 1964. Available through Services Commerciaux de la Réunion des Musées Nationaux, 10 rue de l'Abbaye, Paris.

PARIS

Mobilier National

1, rue Berbier-du-Mets   Metro: Italie
Paris 13e   TEL: 707-10-02

Jean Coural, Administrateur Général
Mme. Muriel de Raïssac, Assistant

The Mobilier National is not a museum in the strict sense of the word, since it seldom holds public exhibits of its collections. It is a national repository for furnishings from the French royal households, and its collections were inherited from the ancient Garde-Meuble Royal and the Mobilier Impérial. It serves as a national archive for examples of the furniture and textiles that decorated the royal palaces at Versailles, Fontainebleau, the Tuilleries, St. Cloud, and Compiègne—among others.

As such its collections are not open to the general public but only to research specialists who wish to study its holdings and to take advantage of the rare documentary material held by its library.

The Mobilier National is housed in a series of somewhat forbidding concrete-block structures surrounding a well-guarded court. (Here also are the headquarters of the Gobelins and Beauvais tapestry works.) To enter, you must pass through a guard house and be admitted by appointment only. Once you enter the executive quarters, however, all is charm and elegance, since the rooms are decorated with furniture and hangings originally meant for the royal palaces.

The Silk Collection

The collection of silk textiles held by the Mobilier National is not large as textile collections go, but it is absolutely dazzling. I mean literally dazzling. The pieces are ablaze with shining silk and yellow-gold thread. At first I could not understand why these 18th- and 19th-Century brocades and damasks were so much more brilliant than similar pieces held by other museums. And then I learned the reason. Most of them are new, never used, though some were woven 250 years ago. When Louis XIV or Napoleon I ordered textiles for one of the royal palaces, only a part of the order was made up into furniture coverings or draperies. The rest was held in reserve for replacements. And it is largely this reserve that Mobilier National owns.

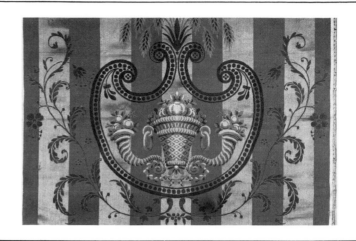

RIGHT. Another piece from the Mobilier collection, a striped satin in shades of green and brown, also dating from the Empire period. Many of these fabrics have never been used. *Mobilier National—GMMP 1658/11 (5468).*

For example, I was shown one piece of silk brocade ordered by Louis XIV to cover the folding stools outside his bedchamber. It was made shortly after the year 1700 by either Chartier or Pernon, two leading silk weavers in Lyon. The design is an ornate arabesque figure in heavy gold thread on a brilliant crimson ground. When it is unrolled, you can hardly believe your eyes. It is so rich, so pristine, that it might have been woven yesterday. (And, indeed, there are still handweavers in Lyon who could achieve this kind of magnificence—but at an incredibly high price.)

Nor is this piece exceptional. The storage cupboards at Mobilier National are crammed with similar pieces. Often there are four coordinated sets of the same basic design, with motifs in different sizes and arrangements for furniture coverings, wall coverings, draperies, and bed valances—valuable documentation for the interior designer.

The total collection of silks (not counting variations on a theme) amounts to 782 pieces, broken down as follows:

18th-Century silks	35
19th-Century silks	587
Empire silks, 1800–1815	160

Most of the Empire silks were ordered from Lyon weavers by Napoleon I in 1806–14. The whole group has been made the subject of a detailed and illustrated study by Jean Coural, Muriel de Raïssac and Chantel Gastinel. It shows that the 160 pieces contain 983 separate design motifs. Information about the availability of the study can be obtained from Mobilier National.

In addition to woven silks the Mobilier also owns a smaller collection of cotton fabrics and printed "Indiennes" made during the first quarter of the 19th Century. A number of them are from the Oberkampf works at Jouy.

The Tapestry Collection

The tapestry collection at Mobilier National is huge—1,010 full-sized works—one of the most extensive in the world. A breakdown of its contents follows, listed by source and period:

TAPESTRIES HELD BY MOBILIER NATIONAL

French Tapestries, 15–16th Century	24 pieces
French Tapestries, 17th Century	84
Foreign Tapestries, chiefly Flemish, plus some from England (Mortlake), Spain, Germany, and Italy.	44
Abbeville Hangings (see note below)	31
Coptic Tapestry Weavings	23
Gobelins Tapestries, 17–18th Century	197
Gobelins Tapestries, 19th Century	55
Gobelins Tapestries, 20th Century	134
Beauvais Tapestries, 18th Century	20
Beauvais Tapestries, 19th Century	79
Beauvais Tapestries, 20th Century	138
Aubusson Tapestries, 16–17th Century	2
Aubusson Tapestries, 18th Century	4
Aubusson Tapestries, 19th Century	29
Aubusson Tapestries, 20th Century	146
TOTAL	1,010 pieces

Abbeville is a small town in the north of France (Somme). It was known for hangings that were woven by machine rather than by hand and in a looser construction than that of traditional tapestry weaving. This group of 31 pieces was made for the coronation of Charles X (1825).

The Rug Collection

The rug collection at Mobilier National is also an important one—475 pieces, of which 370 are of the Savonnerie type. A breakdown follows:

Oriental Rugs (various sources, no inventory available)	105 pieces
Savonnerie Carpets, 17th Century	38
Savonnerie Carpets, 18th Century	26
Savonnerie Carpets, 19th Century	220
Savonnerie Carpets, 20th Century	86
TOTAL	475

*   *   *

Savonnerie is a term used to describe a type of pile carpet with a fine velvety surface (tapis veloutés). They were first made in Paris (Chaillot) about 1620 in a building that had formerly been a soap factory—hence the name.

SENS

Trésor de la Cathédrale
Cathédrale St. Etienne—Place de la République

Abbé Leviste, Curator

There are church treasures throughout France, and some contain textiles both rich and rare—tapestries, burial shrouds, altar cloths, and early ecclesiastical vestments. None, however, are as important or as extensive as the textile treasures in the Cathedral of St. Etienne at Sens.

The cathedral is considered one of the first great structures built on Gothic principles, begun in the year 1130 and consecrated in 1164. It was the Metropolitan Church of Paris, situated 117 km. SE of the capital in the Yonne region. It thus became the repository for many relics.

A number of these relics are ancient textile fragments, buried in anonymous graves or reliquaries and not discovered until 1896. An early inventory of the collection was made by Abbé E. Chartraire and published (with illustrations) in 1897 by A. Picard of Paris and Paul Duchemin of Sens. Unfortunately the work is now out of print and is available only in special libraries. I found it, much annotated, in the library of the Ministère des Affaires Culturelles at 3 rue de Valois in Paris.

The Abbé's inventory lists over 140 textile pieces, some large, others in fragments. A few date from as early as the 6th Century; others from the 8th to the 16th Century. Most are ecclesiastical textiles. Following is a breakdown of the 1896 inventory.

1. Nine tapestries from the 15th and 16th Centuries.

2. Nine shrouds of saints. These are woven, patterned silks dating from the 6th to the 12th Centuries. Perhaps the most important piece in the group is the shroud of the martyr St. Victor. It shows a knight in armor flanked by lions. It is Byzantine in origin, 6th Century.

3. Some 20 silk fragments with patternwork. Most are undated, and the sources unknown, but in the group are pieces from Antinoë in Egypt (4–6th Century) and Syria (6–7th Century).

4. 16 woven silks from Sicily or Italy—12th- and 13th-Century work. Of the group six are also shrouds of saints.

5. 12 medieval pieces from various sources, chiefly oriental in design.

6. Ten fragments of linen and hemp cloth.

7. 12 woven, patterned reliquary bags dating from the 12th, 13th, and 14th Centuries.

8. 25 pieces of early embroidery, some in the form of bags and pouches.

9. 30 liturgical vestments from the 12th Century forwards.

In short, a rare assemblage of medieval fabrics created for the church. And it was the church (together with the nobility) that was patron for the richest and finest work made by medieval weavers and embroiderers.

STRASBOURG

Musée des Arts Décoratifs
Chateau des Rohan
67000 Strasbourg   TEL: 35-29-06

Jean-Daniel Ludmann, Curator

The Strasbourg Musée des Arts Décoratifs—world-renowned for its ceramic collection—owns a modest collection of about 800 historic textiles from Europe, the Middle East, the Far East, and Coptic Egypt. The most substantial representation is from France, Italy, and Germany, with smaller groups from Spain, the Netherlands, Central Europe, Egypt, the Middle East, and the Far East.

Unfortunately, the textile collection has no specialized curator, and the fabrics are held in reserve so that they are accessible only with some difficulty. I am therefore indebted for the following breakdown to M. Ludmann, who is the chief curator of all museum collections in Strasbourg. He prepared the textile inventory especially for this report, with the professional help of Jean Michel Tuchscherer, Curator of the Musée Historique des Tissus in Lyon.

The breakdown follows:

France. About 240 pieces. The most important pieces in this category are 18th-Century woven silks, of which there are some 170 examples. There are also about 30 examples of silk weaving from the 17th and 19th Centuries, as well as 18th-Century velvets, embroideries, and printed cottons.

Italy. About 170 pieces. The largest group includes figured woven silks and velvets dating from the 14th to the 18th Century. The strongest representation is from the

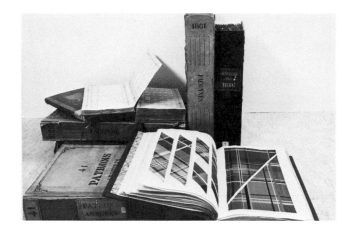

LEFT. One of the two large textiles study rooms at the Centre de Documentation des Fils et Tissus in Tourcoing. The cabinets hold swatch books of 19th- and early 20th-Century fabrics; drawers hold contemporary Jacquards.

RIGHT. Typical 19th-Century swatch books in the Tourcoing collection. Most volumes are clearly labeled by end use and year of production.

16th Century. In addition to woven silks there are embroideries and printed textiles from the 16th Century.

Germany. About 170 pieces. The largest number are embroideries—about 100 pieces dating from the 16th to the 19th Century. There are also examples of silk and velvet weaving from the 17th to the 19th Century, as well as a small group of painted-and-printed cottons.

Spain. About 25 woven silks, velvets, and embroideries of the 16th and 17th Centuries.

Netherlands. Eight pieces of woven, figured silk dating from the 16th and 17th Centuries.

Central Europe. A group of about 40 embroideries on cotton. The work dates from the 18th and 19th Centuries.

Egypt. 13 examples of Coptic tapestry weaving—as yet undated.

Middle East. About 50 pieces. The group includes some 20 woven silks and velvets dating from the 16th to the 19th Century.

Far East. About 75 pieces—18th- and 19th-Century woven silks and embroideries.

TOURCOING

Centre de Documentation des Fils et Tissus
11 bis, Place Charles-Roussel
59200 Tourcoing   TEL: 74-89-16

Mme. Nicole Delannoy, Director

The Tourcoing Centre de Documentation does not consider itself a museum, yet it holds one of the largest textile collections in France. It deserves far greater recognition than it has so far received, since it serves as a fully equipped and practical research facility for professional textile designers, fabric producers, and students of textile design.

The institution was originally founded as a museum. Tourcoing is in the tri-city complex of Lille-Roubaix-Tourcoing, which has long been a manufacturing center for woolen textiles. The three towns are geographically close and form a single industrial region, with one Chamber of Commerce and Industry for the whole area. At the beginning of this century the Chamber acquired a large collection

of historic textiles and opened a Museum of Textile Art & Costume in Tourcoing.

This museum operated until 1960 with one or two exhibitions each year, and the founding collection was continually expanded with gifts of current samples from local textile producers. From 1960–67, however, it ceased operations. In 1968 it was reestablished by the Chamber in its present form as a practical design tool for textile designers and mill owners. It is supported by the Chamber and derives additional income from textile firms, who pay annual membership fees of 1,000 to 2,000 francs for the use of its services.

As a result of annual additions to its original collection given by local textile houses, the Centre now owns some 8,000 examples of historic textiles, plus at least one million swatches. The historic examples range from Coptic tapestry fragments to 19th-Century home-furnishings fabrics. The million swatches chiefly represent 19th- and 20th-Century work, and this latter collection is continually expanding at the rate of about 300 swatches per month—examples of current textile production from France, Switzerland, Italy, the United Kingdom, and the United States. In addition there are 3,000 original textile designs on paper and a collection of French wallpapers for the years 1970–75.

Viewed as a design facility for the textile industry—rather than as a museum—the Centre is unique in France and one of the very few such public facilities anywhere in the world. The only comparable institution that comes to mind is the Design Laboratory at the Fashion Institute of Technology in New York City.

Research Services

The Centre currently offers the following facilities and services to member firms and their design staffs:

1. Historic Textiles—Study Room. This is a large hall on the top floor of the Chamber building overlooking the Place Roussel. In the center of the hall are large work tables. Around the walls are waist-high cabinets with drawers to hold the historic textile collection. There are 27 such cabinets, each with 4 wide drawers—a total of 108 drawers, most of them filled to capacity with textiles in clear plastic covers so they can easily be identified. This is unquestionably one of France's major textile collections by any standard.

Most important for designers is the accessibility of the material. At the Centre there are no obstacles to research.

TOURCOING Continued

Everything in the cabinets may be removed for careful examination, and there is ample work space to spread out the materials.

The range of the historic holdings is wide. Of the 8,000 pieces stored here at least 90% are woven or embroidered, and the rest printed. The following areas have representative coverage:

Coptic tapestry fragments of the 5–6th Centuries. A small token collection.

Gothic textiles of the 15–16th Centuries. A small group from France and Italy.

Renaissance textiles from 16th-Century Italy and Spain. A substantial group of velvets, damasks, and brocades.

French textiles from most major design periods of the 17th to the 19th Centuries—Louis XIII, XIV, Regency, Style Dentelle, Louis XV, 18–19th-Century silks, embroideries, and prints, a large group of woven Cachemires. The biggest group of all (24 drawers) consists of 19th-Century home-furnishings fabrics. The Centre also owns 30 albums of 18th-Century printed swatches from Alsace, with about 1,500 swatches in each album.

An adjoining area of the study hall holds a bank of 11 cabinets with several hundred examples of French costume, mostly 19th-Century work.

All storage facilities are clearly labeled, and the Centre maintains a comprehensive index file of its holdings, classified by period, source, subject, type, style, and technique.

2. Modern Textiles—Study Room. This is another big and well-equipped room in the Chamber building. It has freestanding drawer units for swatches and hanging racks for large pieces, and the walls are lined with large volumes of swatches covering both the 19th and early 20th Centuries. The swatch volumes are labeled according to type or end use—ribbons, cravats, silk dresses, home furnishings, plaids, cotton shirts, prints, etc.

There are about 1,000 such volumes stored in this room and perhaps 1,000 additional volumes held in reserve—a total of about 1,000,000 swatches. Many of them reveal a year-by-year record of 19th-Century styles in wool apparel fabrics for both men and women—a rare and important collection for contemporary designers of outerwear fabrics.

Mme. Delannoy has also been collecting samples of Jacquard fabrics since 1970. She now has several thousand Jacquard swatches that fill 30 drawers in the freestanding cases. They are predominantly home-furnishings fabrics.

Here, as in the historic-textile room, all materials are easily accessible, and there is ample work space.

Design & Color Reference File. The Centre maintains a reference file of design ideas. It is arranged by subject and consists chiefly of clippings taken from international magazines devoted to textiles, fashions, art, and graphics. The file is maintained (with continual additions) as an inspiration for designers who use the Centre in their day-to-day work. The Centre also keeps a continuing record of annual color trends in the textile-apparel markets.

Textile Library. The library is small—about 600 volumes—but it contains interesting works on textile design, technique, and the graphic arts—all geared to the needs of textile designers. The library also has subscriptions to 30 international journals devoted to textiles, fashion, and design.

Photographic Studio. Attached to the textile study rooms is a photographic laboratory equipped to make photographs of any piece in the collection. The Centre has already made photographs of some 1,000 pieces. Negatives are on file, and prints can be made to order. Also on file are about 300 color slides. For photographs of record there is a Polaroid camera and a photocopying machine. The studio is also equipped to make large-scale blowups as a basis for finished textile designs.

Design Service. The Centre employs a full-time artist qualified to make original designs in repeat based on any textile idea or document in the collection. This service is often used by smaller textile producers who do not maintain studios of their own. Such work is paid for by the hour.

Annual Design Expositions. Carrying out its objective of developing a complete design service for the textile industry, the Centre has launched a program called Exposition Internationale de la Création Textile. Its purpose is to invite textile designers and design studios throughout the world to exhibit and sell their designs at a market week attended by textile producers. The first such exposition was held September 24–26, 1975 in Lille under the title Indigo. Participating were 68 designers and design studios from ten countries—France, Germany, England, Spain, Italy, Finland, Holland, Belgium, Sweden, and the U.S.A. Since the Indigo exposition was regarded as a success, the program will probably be continued.

RIGHT. Elegant home of the Musée des Beaux Arts in Tours. The Cathedral of St. Gatien is visible in the background. The museum has a small but important group of Tours silks.

TOURS

Musée des Beaux Arts

18, Place François-Sicard
37000 Tours   TEL: 05-68-73

Mme. Pinot de Villechenon, Curator

Soieries Tourangelles—the silks of Tours. This was a textile name to reckon with until late in the 19th Century. From the 16th Century forward the city of Tours gained an international reputation for the luxury and excellence of its silk weavings. It became a rival of Lyon and was especially famous for Gros de Tours—a heavy silk taffeta made with a double weft, which produced a very strong fabric with an interesting raised-surface texture.

The fame of Tours as a silk-weaving center has now faded, but a modest record of its past achievements is preserved in the elegant Musée des Beaux Arts—a 17th-Century palace of the archbishops that sits among manicured gardens just a stone's throw from the Cathedral of St. Gatien, with its beautiful stained-glass windows.

A brief review of Soieries Tourangelles through the centuries will help to define the role of these silks.

The silk industry of Tours was established in 1466 by a royal decree of Louis XI (reigned 1461–83). Skilled weavers were imported from Lyon and from Italy to make figured silks as well as cloth of gold and silver. The industry prospered and reached a peak during the reign of François I (1515–47). By 1550 the industry was supporting half the population of Tours, which then had 80,000 inhabitants. It produced about 8,000 m. of woven silks each year and employed 20,000 workers in 500 master-weaving workshops. They turned out at least 20 different types of cloth, including brocades, bordered fabrics, figured silks, velvets, moirés, and serges, as well as cloth of gold.

It was a family industry with its own spinning, dyeing, and weaving facilities, but it was dependent on Lyon for its raw silk until 1602. In that year it began to raise its own silkworms in the park of the Château de Plessis-les-Tours.

At the end of the 17th Century the industry declined due to competition from Lyon, continuing wars, and the revocation of the Edict of Nantes (1685), which forced Protestant weavers to emigrate from France.

During the whole of the 18th Century the silk trade went up and down in Tours. Louis XIV favored Lyon over Tours; Louis XV favored Tours over Lyon. But during the last third of the 18th Century the city achieved its finest silk weavings and its fabrics were held in high esteem.

Until the Revolution (1789) Tours continued to be a royal manufactory of velvets and damasks. After 1790 it declined during the suppression of corporations, and not until 1819 was a new silk plant established in the city. Throughout the 19th Century Soieries Tourangelles prospered again, specializing in luxurious Jacquards and achieving a worldwide reputation for both quality and design.

A somewhat meager though not uninteresting record of this illustrious textile history is now preserved by the city. Unfortunately, it is only a small collection, and at this writing it is not on public display. There are plans to expand the holdings in the future and to give them permanent exhibit space in several galleries of the museum. Until that time, however, the collection is accessible only to specialists and by appointment.

Extent of the Collection

In all, the Musée des Beaux Arts now holds about 420 pieces, representing most phases of the city's silk history except early work of the 15th Century. The collection breaks down into two categories:

1. Pieces of Silk. There are about 120 examples. A number are full-repeat lengths rolled on tubes. The remainder are large swatches mounted on cards. They cover a time span from the 16th to the 19th Centuries. About 70 pieces date from the 16th to the 18th Centuries, and 50 pieces are 19th-Century work. Examples of Gros de Tours cover the whole time span. There are also samples of gold cloth, damask, brocatelle, brocade, satin, and costume pieces.

2. Designs on Paper. This is perhaps the main asset of the textile collection. It consists of 300 silk designs, chiefly 18th- and 19th-Century work, many of them on graph paper. The 18th-Century designs (in aquarelle and gouache) were made by students at the Ecole de Dessin de Tours, founded by A. Rougeot. The 19th-Century work comes mainly from two famous designers—Grandbarbe and César Galais. In some cases both the original design and the fabric made from it are owned by the museum.

NOTE. The Bibliothèque Nationale in Paris owns a collection of five large volumes containing swatches of Soieries Tourangelles and designs on paper—all made between 1720 and 1750 (*Cabinet des Estampes, Lh 44-44d*).

Le Médecin dans la Poche, a printed scarf designed by Buquet about 1880 and produced by the firm of E. Renault in Rouen. *Musée de l'Impression sur Etoffes, Mulhouse.*

COLOR SECTION

A 32-page color sampling from French textile collections begins on the facing page.

FRANCE. Alsatian textile print design in gouache or paper, made by Atelier Schaub of Mulhouse. Schaub was a leading design studio for regional textile printers during the late 19th Century. It turned out superb flower prints like the ones shown here and on the next page. The Musée de l'Impression sur Etoffes in Mulhouse owns a unique record of some 500 Schaub designs on paper in addition to examples of printed textiles designed by the same studio. *Mulhouse—258.*

TOP. **FRANCE.** 18th-Century silk embroidery for man's waistcoat. Louis XVI (1754–93). *Lyon—35118/2.*

LEFT. **FRANCE.** Print design by Atelier Schaub of Mulhouse, late 19th C. Gouache on paper. *Mulhouse—36E.*

RIGHT. **FRANCE.** Home-furnishings print made 1854–56. Gift of Haurez. *Mulhouse—S.1053, p. 88.*

FRANCE. Textile print design, gouache on paper, made 1850–80 in Mulhouse. Gift of Thierry-Mieg. *Mulhouse—S.1176, p. 4683.*

FRANCE. Paper strikeoff from a textile print plate by unknown Mulhouse printer, 1860. *Mulhouse—No Number.*

LEFT. **FRANCE.** Alsatian print design on paper, 1850–60. Gift of Thierry-Mieg. *Mulhouse—S.1176, p. 4678.*

RIGHT. **FRANCE.** Woodblock border print on cotton made by Oberkampf at Jouy, 1780. *Mulhouse—858.283.1.*

TOP LEFT. **FRANCE.** Cut velvet in five colors, early 18th C. *Paris, Musée des Arts Décoratifs—9496A.*

TOP RIGHT. **FRANCE.** Brocaded silk lampas, Regency (1715–23). *Paris, Musée des Arts Décoratifs—9476.*

BOTTOM LEFT. **FRANCE.** Six-color cut velvet, early 18th Century. *Paris, Musée des Arts Décoratifs—20786.*

BOTTOM RIGHT. **FRANCE.** Cut velvet, ground embroidered with pearls, Louis XV (1715–74). *Lyon—2234.*

LEFT. **ITALY.** Multicolored cut velvet, 17th Century. *Lyon—24683/2.*

TOP. **FRANCE.** Cut velvet, about 1700. *Paris, Musée des Arts Décoratifs—2409.*

BOTTOM. **FRANCE.** Brocaded silk, Louis XV, about 1740–50. *Paris, Musée des Arts Décoratifs—10469.*

LEFT. **FRANCE.** Detail of a hanging, brocaded-silk lampas, designed by Philippe de Lasalle (1723–1803) and woven at Lyon in 1771 for Catherine of Russia. *Lyon—1278.*

TOP. **FRANCE.** Brocaded silk by Lasalle, late 18th C., for Marie Antoinette at Fontainbleau. *Lyon—28627.*

BOTTOM. **FRANCE.** *Toilette de Vénus.* Printed toile by Favre Petitpierre of Nantes, 1790. Made with a combination of copperplate and woodblock printing (for the color accents). *Mulhouse—954.413.1.*

TOP LEFT. **ITALY.** Brocaded satin, 16th Century. *Lyon—No Number.*

TOP RIGHT. **FRANCE.** Brocaded silk, Tours, Louis XV (1715–74). *Paris, Musée des Arts Décoratifs—13260.*

BOTTOM LEFT. **FRANCE.** Louis XV brocaded-silk lampas in the à dentelle style. *Lyon—2862.*

BOTTOM RIGHT. **FRANCE.** Louis XV brocaded taffeta, 1740–50. *Paris, Musée des Arts Décoratifs—9470.*

TOP. **EGYPT.** *Triumph of the Cross.* Coptic bouclé weave, 9th Century, 120 ×210 cm. *Louvre—AC927.*

LEFT. **EGYPT.** Coptic wool-linen tapestry fragment, 5th Century, 147 × 26 cm. *Louvre—X4192 (B27).*

CENTER. **EGYPT.** Coptic wool-linen tapestry detail, 6th Century, 57 × 37 cm. *Louvre—MG1229 (T49).*

RIGHT. **EGYPT.** Coptic portrait, wool-linen tapestry weave, 23 × 21 cm. *Louvre—X4631 (F231).*

TOP LEFT. **EGYPT.** Coptic dancer's head, 5th Century, tapestry weave, 42 × 32 cm. *Louvre—X4849 (B22).*

TOP RIGHT. **EGYPT.** *Aphrodite,* Coptic tapestry fragment, 6th Century, 27 × 26 cm. *Louvre—X4151 (C76).*

LEFT. **EGYPT.** *Dionysius,* Coptic tapestry fragment, 7th Century, 58 × 55 cm. *Louvre—X4792 (B24).*

CENTER. **EGYPT.** Coptic tapestry detail, 6th Century, 25 × 20 cm. *Louvre—E28172 (MG104).*

RIGHT. **EGYPT.** Coptic tapestry detail of pomegranates, 8th Century, 37 × 18 cm. *Louvre—X4780 (D145).*

EGYPT. One of the outstanding pieces in the Musée Historique des Tissus at Lyon. It is a wool-tapestry fragment (140 × 87 cm) recovered from the graves at Antinoë in 1907–8. The museum currently describes it as Egypt—Coptic Period, which would date it at the earliest in the 1st Century A.D. But the museum's 1929 catalog dated it B.C. and speculated that it might have been woven on a Mediterranean Greek island. A smaller fragment from the same or a similar piece is on display in the Louvre's Coptic Galleries, dated 2–3rd Century A.D. *Lyon—28927.*

EGYPT. An equally charming but more characteristic Coptic piece from the Lyon collection is shown approximately actual size (21 × 20 cm). It is a funerary cushion cover dated 3–4th Century A.D. and is tapestry-woven in wool on ecru linen. Both the colors and the construction are remarkably well preserved. The figure of the hare or rabbit is frequently seen in early Coptic pieces. *Lyon—24409.*

EGYPT. One of two companion Coptic tapestry weaves from the Greco-Roman period, 4–5th Century A.D. It is a funerary cover found in the graves at Antinoë and is 29 cm square—or about 25% larger than shown here. The companion piece has a cavalier in the central circle instead of a centaur, as here. Both pieces are woven in multi-colored wools on an ecru linen ground. *Lyon—24423.*

TOP. **EGYPT.** The sacrifice of Isaac by Abraham. A Coptic tapestry weaving of the 5th Century A.D. reflecting Byzantine influence. It is 12 × 26 cm in size. *Lyon—24400/55.*

LEFT. **EGYPT.** Coptic tapestry weave, possibly of the 5th Century A.D. *Lyon—24563/6.*

RIGHT. **EGYPT.** A Coptic tapestry decoration of the 6th Century A.D. showing Byzantine-Sassanid inspiration. It was recovered from the graves at Fayoum. Height is 33 cm. *Lyon—24412.*

TOP LEFT. **BYZANTINE.** Heavy silk hanging of the 7–8th Century. *Lyon—22628.*

TOP RIGHT. **EGYPT.** Coptic wool *Alexander* tapestry from Antinoë, 7–8th Century. *Lyon—28928.*

BOTTOM LEFT. **ANATOLIA** (Ushak). Rug made with Gordian knots. End of 16th Century. *Lyon—MAD 150.*

BOTTOM RIGHT. **PERSIA.** 11th-Century tapestry from St. Géréon Church, Cologne. *Lyon—22963.*

TOP. **PERSIA.** Brocaded cut velvet, 17th Century. About 32 cm wide. *Lyon—29724.*

BOTTOM. **BYZANTINE.** Silk hanging, 8–10th Century, from church of Mozac (Puy de Dôme). *Lyon—27386.*

RIGHT. **PERSIA.** Velvetlike knotted rug of Tibetan wool (almost as fine as silk), enhanced with gold and silver threads. A superb example of rugmaking from end of 16th Century. 185 × 280 cm. *Lyon—25700.*

JAVA. Unusual colorings in a Javanese batik of the 19th Century. *Mulhouse—954.48.1.*

TOP LEFT. **PERSIA.** Printed hanging or bed cover made about 1800. *Mulhouse—858.144.1.*

TOP RIGHT. **PERSIA.** Mordant-painted and dyed cover, made about 1780. *Mulhouse—118527.*

BOTTOM LEFT. **JAVA.** Traditional colorings in a Javanese batik of the 19th Century. *Mulhouse—No Number.*

BOTTOM RIGHT. **PERSIA.** Border of mordant-painted and dyed cover, end of 18th Century. *Mulhouse—967.189.1.*

FRANCE. A tour de force of woodblock printing by the Alsatian printer Ch. Steiner of Ribeauvillé. It was made in 1900 for the International Exposition held that year in Paris. The panel is titled *Chinoiseries* and was designed by Martin et Couder of Paris. It was executed in 18 colors and required over 800 block impressions. *Mulhouse—No Number.*

LEFT. **JAPAN.** Detail of a silk tapestry woven in the 19th Century. *Lyon—32,600.*

RIGHT. **TIBET.** 19th-Century silk temple banner with appliqué design of symbolic religious figures. The background fabric is woven silk imported from China.

CAMBODIA. A superb example of the Indonesian weft ikat from the latter part of the 19th Century. The cloth, including solid-color side borders not shown, is over seven feet long. *Mulhouse—966.91.1.*

TOP. **SUMBA.** One half (about 1.4 m.) of an early 20th-Century weft ikat from this Indonesian island. The other half is a mirror image of the section shown. *Paris, Musée de l'Homme—55.68.55 (8012).*

BOTTOM. **CAMBODIA.** Another example of a late 19th-Century weft ikat. The cloth is over seven feet long, and about 60% of the design is shown here. The same motifs are repeated in the rest of the cloth. *Mulhouse—954.515.1.*

LEFT. **U.S.S.R.** Uzbek woman's robe of silk ikat from Bukhara. The garment is 90 × 124 cm., not counting the sleeves. It was probably made in the late 19th Century. *Paris, Musée de l'Homme—67.110.270 (8031).*

RIGHT. **AFGHANISTAN.** Contemporary cotton ikat from the province of Jozjan, village of Qumarigh. It was made in 1973. *Paris, Musée de l'Homme—975.22.332 (8013).*

LEFT. **DAHOMEY** (Abomey). Cotton-appliqué hanging, formerly used as decoration for a chief's house. It depicts the cutting of coconut palm. 1.76 × 1 m. *Paris, Musée de l'Homme—36.21.21 (8007).*

RIGHT. **VIETNAM** (Annam). Woven-cotton cover or skirt with motifs called *Isles of the Ocean.* From the Da Döng region, Döng-Nai basin. 118.5 × 78 cm. *Paris, Musée de l'Homme—62.91.9 (2746).*

DAHOMEY. Embroidered-cotton tunic, 90 cm. in length and 50 cm. at the shoulders. A royal ceremonial costume. *Paris, Musée de l'Homme—36.21.102 (8006).*

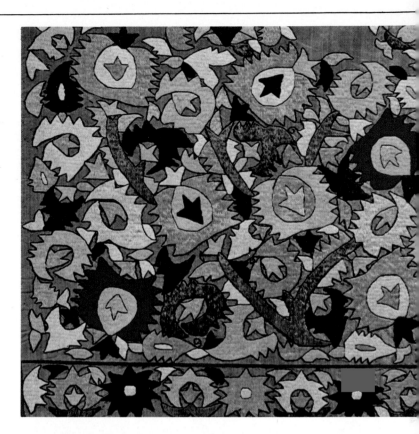

TOP LEFT. **TURKEY.** (Konya). Wool rug (*Garden of Aranos*). *Paris, Musée de l'Homme—973.77.182 (6318).*

TOP RIGHT. **MOROCCO** (Tetuan). Silk-embroidered sash, 37 × 33 cm. *Paris, Musée de l'Homme—67.33.24 (8009).*

BOTTOM LEFT. **AFGHANISTAN** (Fariab). 20th-C. cotton embroidery. *Paris, Musée de l'Homme—67.110.250 (7674).*

BOTTOM RIGHT. **IRAK** (Mossul). Detail of silk-embroidered garment. *Paris, Musée de l'Homme—67.100.77 (8008).*

NORWAY. 18th-Century wool tapestry. *Paris, Musée de l'Homme—90.35.2 (8011).*

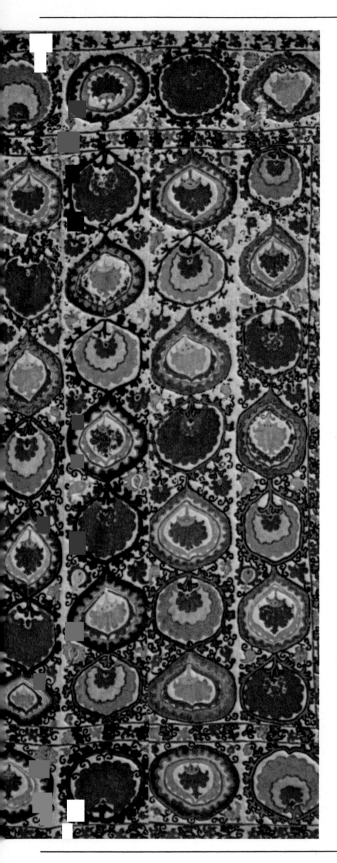

LEFT. **U.S.S.R.** Section of Uzbek hanging in embroidered cotton from Bukhara, early 19th Century. Overall size, 180 × 240 cm.; each vertical band, 27 cm. wide. *Paris, Musée de l'Homme—67.110.253 (7676).*

RIGHT. **YUGOSLAVIA.** Woman's embroidered robe, Timok, E. Serbia. *Paris, Musée de l'Homme—55.59.452 (8010).*

ENGLAND. *Woman with Daisy* by the Art Nouveau Czechoslovakian designer Alphonse Mucha (1860–1939). Printed on velveteen by the London firm of Hines, Stroud & Co. in 1899–1900. *Paris, Bibliothèque Forney—A554.*

TOP LEFT. **FRANCE.** Textile design in gouache by E. A. Seguy, 1924. *Paris, Bibliothèque Forney—105866.*

TOP RIGHT. **FRANCE.** Art Deco design in gouache by M. P. Verneuil, 1927. *Paris, Bibliothèque Forney—100925.*

BOTTOM LEFT. **FRANCE.** Art Deco gouache design by Buchalter, 1928–31. *Paris, Bibliothèque Forney—114454.*

BOTTOM RIGHT. **FRANCE.** Art Deco design in gouache by Gladky, 1931. *Paris, Bibliothèque Forney—110504.*

FRANCE. *Les Allies.* A silk commemorative scarf (40 × 40 cm.) designed by Raoul Dufy in 1915 and printed by wood-block at the firm of Ferret in St. Denis. It was issued by the Atelier Martine (P. Poiret) of Paris. *Mulhouse—961.701.1.M.*

THE TEXTILE TRADITIONS OF FRANCE

Monique Toury-King
Conservateur des Musées Nationaux de France
Formerly of the Musée du Louvre & Musée de Cluny, Paris

ANTIQUITY & MIDDLE AGES

Woven Fabrics

France has a climate which, like that of other countries in Western Europe, is favorable to the production of wool and flax. These two textile fibers were woven in Gaul back in classical times. Fabrics with stripes or simple motifs were manufactured in the Midi. Plain, thick woolens, to be made into capes, were exported from Gaul to Rome and elsewhere. The Romans themselves set up a number of imperial workshops in the Midi (Lyon), and in the North (Reims).

The wool-weaving industry grew in importance during the Middle Ages; some of the processed wool used was fine wool imported from England. In the 13th and 14th Centuries Abbeville, Amiens, Arras, Caen, Cambrai, Douai, Lille, Paris, Provins, Saint-Omer, Saint-Quentin, and Valenciennes exported many kinds of wool cloth throughout the whole of Europe and the Islamic world. It amounted to a capitalistic enterprise with its subsidiary industries: preparation of the fibers before weaving; dyeing, which was an industry in and of itself, with the quality of the color an important element in the value of the cloth; and finishing, which, for wool, involved many complex operations. Linen weaving continued to be practiced in the same regions, and the fine linens of Reims enjoyed an international reputation. There still remain—as in the cathedral of Sens—fragments of decorative linen from the High Middle Ages, possibly manufactured in France.

As early as the High Middle Ages France imported large quantities of silks, both plain and patterned, from the Byzantine Empire, from the Islamic countries, from Spain, and later from Italy. Some of those—in the treasury of the Sens cathedral and in the Paris and Lyon museums—represent four-legged animals and birds. During the Middle Ages silk weaving was practiced in France only on a very small scale.

Trade in textiles occurred chiefly at fairs, where most of the import and export business was carried on. The most famous were those of Champagne and Lyon, to which merchants came from all over Europe and the East.

Embroidery

Fragments of French medieval embroidery have survived proportionately better than those of other textile techniques. Paris was the principal center. Bands embroidered with gold rosettes decorate the sleeves of a silk tunic dating from the 6th Century recently discovered in Saint-Denis. A linen garment from Chelles, dating from the 7th or 8th Century, is decorated with silk embroidery representing necklaces and with a gold cross inlaid with jewels. The most important of all the embroideries from the Middle Ages, the Bayeux Tapestry—depicting in a long frieze the conquest of England by the Normans in 1066—is often considered an English work but could well have been executed in Normandy.

French embroidery of the Gothic period does not have the same reputation as the Opus Anglicanum of England. However there do remain a number of superb religious pieces worked in gold and silk threads, such as the copes of Montiéramey and Saint-Maximin; the altar-front panels at Château-Thierry, at the Toulouse museum and at the Cathedral of Sens; and the miters at the Cluny and Evreux museums. Charming purses embroidered in gold and silk and representing amorous couples are typical of 14th-Century art. The Chartres museum preserves a religious triptych, a beautiful example of embroidery dating from the beginning of the 15th Century.

Tapestries

The weaving of large wall hangings, done in wool tapestry, was practiced in Paris at the end of the 14th Century. The great Apocalypse tapestries, preserved in the Château of Angers and woven between 1373 and 1379 by Nicolas Bataille, are marvelous examples of such weaving. But it was Arras and Tournai, then a French enclave, that produced the beautiful tapestries of the Middle Ages, representing pastoral scenes or subjects either sacred or romantic. They are still to be found in large numbers in museums and cathedrals.

Perhaps the most attractive are the mille-fleurs, in which the background depicts a meadow dotted with wildflowers. Of such the most famous are *The Lady with the Unicorn* tapestries at the Cluny Museum in Paris.

17th & 18th CENTURIES

Wool, Flax, and Cotton

Wool and flax weaving continued to be one of the main activities of many cities in the North and in Normandy. The wool cloths of Rouen, Dreux, Dieppe, Beauvais, Elbeuf, Sedan, Falaise, as well as those of Neuilly and Orléans,

are celebrated. Dozens of other centers throughout France specialized in various types of woolens. In 1663 Colbert brought fifty craftsmen to Abbeville from Holland under the direction of Josse van Robais in order to manufacture woolen cloth by Dutch methods.

Linen cloth was produced in the North as well as in Normandy. Since the 16th Century linen damask has been the specialty of Courtrai, now a part of Belgium but French for a short period at the time when Colbert reorganized the textile industry.

Cotton, imported from the East, spread throughout the European market in the 16th Century. Striped cotton fabrics with linen or silk warps (called Siamese) began to be produced at Rouen in 1649.

Silk ribbons became a specialized industry in Paris, Lyon, Saint-Chamond, and Saint-Etienne.

Some of these materials, ranging from the most common to the most luxurious, were exported. Trade in fabrics of all kinds took place at fairs, which were held throughout the kingdom. Among the most famous were those at Beaucaire, Caen, the Lendit fair at Saint-Denis, and those at Lyon. Naturally, all kinds of luxury fabrics were to be found at the merchant houses in Paris.

Silks: Lyon

While Lyon, with a monopoly of the Italian silk trade, became immensely rich, King Louis XI worried about this great drain of gold and silver from the kingdom and tried to introduce in France the weaving of luxury silks. In 1466 he attempted unsuccessfully to impose on the inhabitants of Lyon, at their expense, the installation of Italian workshops.

In 1470 the workshops were transferred to Tours near the royal residence. The beginnings were modest, but in the middle of the 16th Century Tours could boast of two or three thousand looms. Immediately Lyon became interested and in 1536 obtained from Francis I, on his return from Italy, the grants needed for setting up Italian weavers in Lyon.

Lyon and Tours were not alone. Workshops sprang up everywhere; Avignon, Saint-Etienne, Rouen, Paris, and Carpentras also produced silks. The demand for them was enormous because, despite hard times, styles in clothing were unbelievably extravagant. But only silks that were plain or with small designs came from the French looms. The Italians still dominated the market for figured silks, which were imported in substantial quantities.

With the accession of Henry IV a policy of economic recovery was inaugurated. Olivier de Serres and Barthélémy Laffemas conducted a virtual crusade to plant mulberry trees, essential to the culture of silkworms. At the same time the silk industry was supported and encouraged. Tours, which benefited from Richelieu's patronage, and Lyon, where improvements in the looms made by Claude Dangon allowed daring techniques, grew by leaps and bounds. But it was due to Colbert's economic policies that, around 1660, the complete reorganization of the textile industry, ensuring homogeneity and quality of production, soon permitted France to compete with Italy and eventually to dominate the international market.

Tours and Lyon were in full swing along with many other centers of production. A workshop near Paris wove immensely rich silks for Versailles. However, the French silks did not yet differ from the Italian ones on which they were modeled so that the dating of existing materials and their attribution to France are of necessity tentative. Many fabrics traditionally called Louis XIII are really neither French nor from the 17th Century.

The techniques in Italy and France were the same: brocaded lampas gold or silver lamé on a damask background with a secondary design as counterpoint to the main one—brocaded velvet enhanced with motifs of bouclé velvet, etc. The designs were of two types, which originated in Italy during the 15th and 16th Centuries: symmetrical compositions of fleurons, pomegranates, wreaths, birds, and stylized vases or a scattering of twigs, bouquets, and plants in alternating and inclined rows.

Fabrics considered to be French can be identified by slender but extremely effective designs in which the repetition of the motif is masked by the skill of the composition, while the flora become progressively more naturalistic. At the same time fabrics with small designs were undoubtedly manufactured in many places besides Tours and Lyon. These fabrics, with minor concessions to fashion, were to be produced until the 19th Century.

At the end of Louis XIV's reign (1643–1715) economic, political, and even religious crises, such as the repression of the Huguenots, had repercussions in the silk industry. Tours, with many Huguenots, suffered especially, leaving Lyon without a rival. Foreign competition increased. England and Holland produced quality silks more and more

FAR LEFT. French embroidered bag, 13th Century, 14.5 cm. wide. *Musée des Arts Décoratifs, Paris—16330 (5023)*.

LEFT. French embroidered casket, 18th Century, 25 cm. long. *Musée des Arts Décoratifs, Paris—37149 (7822)*.

RIGHT. Design on paper for woven silk, early Louis 14th (1643–1715). *Musée des Beaux Arts, Tours—IH190 (17553-4)*.

closely inspired by French models, but Italy remained especially strong in fabrics for interiors.

However, the demand also increased enormously, and after the Treaty of Utrecht in 1713, which opened foreign markets to French trade, there began for Lyon a period of great prosperity. In this climate technical progress went hand in hand with the quality of design. The many competent and highly regarded Lyon designers went to Paris every year to study fashion and brought back new, up-to-date designs. Paris set the style for all of Europe. Naturally, inventions flourished: bizarre silks (at the turn of the century) with surrealist or exotic motifs, gold and silver fabrics for waistcoats, striped silks with tiny flowers, brocaded damasks with bold, symmetrical floral patterns, lampas with large flowers in full bloom such as those designed by Jean Ravel around 1730.

Toward the middle of the century forms became more graceful. The most frequent theme consisted of a vertical, sinuous band with intertwined plants and flowers. The band could be ribbon, lace, fur, stem, tree trunk, or garland. It could crisscross to form a trellis. As the century progressed, colors became lighter, while the motifs, which were more delicate, more discreet and stylized, seemed to be created to enhance the value of the background material and not to dominate it completely.

This was also the period when Philippe de Lasalle produced his magnificent interior fabrics put out in limited editions for a royal clientele. Under Marie Antoinette the demand for figured silks decreased considerably. Fashion favored light fabrics, and printed cottons were the rage. Only court clothes still required heavy brocaded silks. Even before the outbreak of the Revolution, which for several years paralyzed the industry in Lyon, it was chiefly plain or small-motif silks that came from the Lyon looms. The most glorious period of the French silk industry had ended.

It was Napoleon's policy that restored the industry in Lyon. Through the reorganization of the profession, and especially through imperial orders, the industry was revived. The court was under orders to dress in silks from Lyon. Saint-Cloud, Versailles, Compiègne, Fontainebleau, and the Tuileries were redecorated according to the current fashion. Naturally, the satellite courts of Europe followed suit. Clothes were almost always of plain silk or velvet trimmed with embroidery, but upholstery materials in the official martial style—symmetrical, severe, and with a return to antiquity—had an unquestioned grandeur and a superb technical quality.

Printed Fabrics: Jouy, Alsace

In the middle of the 17th Century the painted fabrics from India, called Indiennes, enjoyed a great popularity in France as elsewhere in Europe. It was not long before attempts were made to imitate them. The silk manufacturers, who feared this competition, obtained royal edicts forbidding the importation and the manufacture of Indiennes. As a result it was in Switzerland, Alsace, Holland, England, and Germany that the techniques of printing on cotton were developed, making possible the replacement at a lower cost of the real hand-painted Indiennes. Finally, in 1759, when the prohibition was removed, workshops were established everywhere with the help of technicians from foreign countries.

The most famous among these was the workshop of Oberkampf, a Bavarian, who set up at Jouy, near Versailles. His workshop, which soon became prosperous, was favored by Marie Antoinette and her court. Jean-Baptiste Huet, over a period of thirty years, furnished this workshop with its most celebrated designs. Some were pleasant pastoral scenes after Boucher. Others, bearing on current events, were toiles such as: *Departure of the Montgolfier Balloon Federation Day, Homage from America to France.*

While these large subjects were being engraved on copperplates, small designs were produced on woodcuts for upholstery and dress materials. In the same period innumerable factories sprang up and had a more or less brief existence. The best were in Rouen, Nantes, Orléans, and Orange. Alsace, which had escaped the prohibition, had more than twenty establishments. Production was enormous and varied: not only country scenes as at Jouy but also an infinite number of graceful and light floral compositions following very closely the styles in silk.

Jouy was not affected by the Revolution. Quite the contrary. The invention of roller printing made possible a great increase in production. The Emperor and all the learned men of the time were interested in the manufacturing process. Huet succeeded in adapting his style to the official taste without losing any of its pleasing grace. However, the death of Oberkampf and the fall of the Empire put an end to the Jouy workshop.

Lace

Lace had its origin in Italy at the end of the 15th Century. Starting with the 16th Century, the Italian and Flemish laces enjoyed a strong vogue in France. In the 17th Century

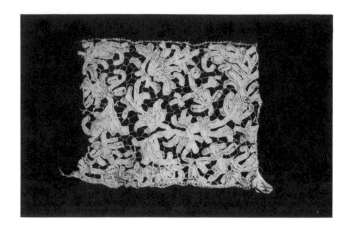

TEXTILE TRADITIONS Continued

they became the rage. Large collars and lace jabots adorned men's clothes and were worn even on suits of armor. Albs and surplices of the high clergy were trimmed with it. Women wore aprons, collars, and hair ornaments made of lace.

In 1661 Colbert founded the Royal Lace Manufactures. Italian and Flemish lace makers were imported. French artists were given commissions to furnish designs. Workshops for needle lace were established in Alençon, Argentan, and Sedan. The Point de France at first imitated the Point de Venise, but beginning in 1690 the designs were composed around architectural elements after Bérain.

At the beginning of the 18th Century patterns became more flexible and sinuous, with bizarre or exotic elements. It was the most beautiful period. Around 1750 they became thin and spindly, and by 1770 lace was no longer in style. At the same time bobbin lace had spread from Flanders to France starting in the 17th Century. Valenciennes worked in the Antwerp style. At the end of the 18th Century workshops were operating in Lille, Arras, Le Puy, and Chantilly.

Tapestries: Gobelins, Beauvais, and Aubusson

During the Renaissance French tapestry workshops were eclipsed by the glory of those in Brussels, which had a reputation all over Europe. Once again the credit goes to Colbert for the creation of the Royal Manufacture of the Gobelins in 1663. He grouped together the excellent workshops that existed in the Paris region and reorganized them under the direction of Charles Le Brun, First Painter to the King. The factory produced hangings for the royal palaces and for diplomatic gifts. They were based on cartoons by the best painters of the period: Le Brun, Audran, Desportes, Van Der Meulen, and Boucher. Colbert was also responsible for the factory in Beauvais, which for the most part served a private clientele, producing graceful hangings as well as upholstery, screens, and portières designed by Bérain, Boucher, and Audry.

Several workshops have been in existence in Aubusson since the 16th Century and are still operating to this day. In the 17th and 18th Centuries they not only produced verdures (tapestries with plant-ornament or landscape subjects) but also imitated in a more rustic style the products of Paris and Beauvais.

Rugs: Savonnerie, Aubusson

Oriental rugs have been admired, imported, and perhaps even imitated in France since the Middle Ages. But the origins of Savonnerie rugs date from the beginning of the 17th Century when two workshops under the aegis of the king were set up in Paris for the production of "Turkish" rugs. One was in a former soap (savon) factory; the other, in the Louvre. Colbert's reform in 1663 made the Savonnerie workshop a Royal Manufacture under the direction of Charles Le Brun.

In the 18th Century the workshops were transferred to the buildings of the Gobelins Manufacture, but the Savonnerie plant worked only for the Crown, which meant that both quality and price were very high. The creation of rug factories under royal patronage at Aubusson (from 1743 on) was developed to achieve more abundant production and a quality more within reach. During the reign of Louis XIV the Savonnerie rugs had magnificent, symmetrical designs around a large central motif with a bold pattern and large-scale compositions. Under Louis XV designs at Aubusson and at Savonnerie became roccoco, graceful, light, and naturalistic. Napoleon took a lively interest in the revival of the two factories. With the impetus given by Royal Architects Percier and Fontaine, the palaces were furnished with immense rugs displaying huge compositions in the style of the reign.

Embroidery

Embroidery was made in France throughout the Old Regime, especially in Paris and near the court in Touraine, at Fontainebleau, and at Versailles. In fact, not only clothes but also interior furnishings were enriched with embroidery: beds, hangings, portières, curtains, and upholstery. At Versailles Louis XIV's study included 15-foot-high caryatids in relief, executed in gold and silver embroidery. In the 18th Century men's coats and waistcoats were a particular specialty of Lyon. They were embroidered in such a way that the tailor could cut and assemble them to fit. Embroidery was also very much in demand for ecclesiastical needs. Cathedrals and churches even to this day have a large number of liturgical pieces, gifts of bishops and kings of the 17th and 18th Centuries, made in Paris and Lyon.

The art of embroidery was also practiced by amateurs almost everywhere in France. The Saint-Cyr school founded by Madame de Maintenon, many charity workshops, and numerous convents produced lay or religious

FAR LEFT. French brocaded taffeta, Regency period (1715–23). *Musée Historique des Tissus, Lyon—29575.*

LEFT. French imitation of Point de Venise lace, 12 × 15 cm. Type made by Mme. de la Perrière. *Musée d'Oze, Alençon.*

RIGHT. French woven wool *Cachemire*, made about 1850. *Centre de Documentation des Fils et Tissus, Tourcoing—146.*

embroideries that occasionally were of remarkable quality. The favorite motifs of embroiderers from the Renaissance on were seldom pictorial, as they were in the Middle Ages, but rather ornamental: whorls, foliated scrolls, and especially plants and flowers. Under Louis XVI and during the Empire, embroidery was used especially for the enhancement of plain fabrics, which were then in vogue. Clothes and hangings were decorated with bucolic motifs in the taste of Trianon or with trophies, sphinxes, and flags in the style of antiquity.

THE 19th CENTURY

Increasing mechanization began to transform the textile industry in the 19th Century. Equipment became more complex, production more intense, and the finished product cheaper. Quantity was thereby increased, but naturally artistic quality became secondary.

Jacquard, a citizen of Lyon invented the loom that bears his name and that was a major advance in the production of figured fabrics. The whole textile production of the 19th Century was characterized by technical virtuosity and the decline of inventiveness. Designs were more often than not derivative. Pompadour, Trianon, and Empire were exploited remorselessly, especially when it came to rugs and upholstery materials, either woven or printed.

As for clothing, the demand for plain or figured fabrics did not decrease. Quite the contrary. Fashions of the Romantic Period, of the Second Empire, or of the Belle Epoque compelled women to dress in elaborate and frothy clothes. Crinolines in particular required vast quantities of material. During the Second Empire, court and ball gowns displayed large-scale and complicated compositions in which flowers and garlands, drapery, and trompe-l'oeil lace were spread in profusion.

At the end of the 18th Century the shawl became an indispensable accessory. It could be plain or figured, embroidered, made of wispy lace or thick wool. It dressed the rich and the poor. The beautiful shawls of Kashmir were very much admired and quickly imitated. In France compositions of extraordinary complexity, inspired by Indian shawls, were woven on Jacquard looms. Silk ones came from Lyon; wool shawls from Paris; and some printed on cotton came from Alsace.

Lace was very popular and stunning in technical quality whether it was completely handmade, just hand-worked on a base of machine-made net, or produced on the Jacquard loom, especially in Lyon and Calais. Black lace called Chantilly (although manufactured in Bayeux since 1830) was especially prized at the end of the century.

Embroidery was used abundantly for dresses and accessories: purses, gloves, handkerchiefs, and underwear. It was not only done professionally. Skill with the needle was found in all classes of society.

Tapestry, whether at Gobelins, Beauvais, or Aubusson, was limited to the reproduction of old cartoons, to the copying of museum paintings, or to the representation of large historical events taken from cartoons supplied by generally mediocre painters. The technical skill of the tapestry weavers and the unlimited range of available colors allowed the almost perfect reproduction of paintings without any regard for the values inherent in a tapestry.

THE 20th CENTURY

At the end of the 19th Century we find attempts to infuse the industrial arts with the new spirit then transforming the fine arts. There were many talented painters who took an active interest in the textile arts and tried to produce designs adapted to their function and to the medium in which they were carried out. Among the most famous artists or promoters one must cite Maillol, Charles Dufrène, Paul Iribe, Paul Poiret, and Raoul Dufy.

Tapestry did not escape this movement, but it is Jean Lurçat and Marcel Gromaire who deserve credit for its virtual renaissance since the last war. Matisse, Picart Le Doux, Marc Saint-Saens, Dom Robert, and many others furnished Aubusson, Gobelins, and other workshops with cartoons that show a tremendous concern for forms and colors and a conscious return to the aesthetics of the medieval tapestry.

Rugs also benefited from this movement, and the Savonnerie and Aubusson workshops produced pieces of striking simplicity.

Today the introduction of artificial fibers has revolutionized the whole textile industry. Lyon had to adapt itself but still produces silks on a very small scale and remains unequaled in the reproduction of antique fabrics required for the restoration of historical residences.

Translation from the French by Marguerite and Don Miles

French satin with design motif in metallic yarn, woven about 1920. *Musée Historique des Tissus, Lyon—34830.*

TEXTILE DESIGN IDEAS

The black-and-white photographs that follow—together with the color section that preceded—offer a representative sampling of textiles held by French museums. The largest proportion of them are French textiles, reflecting the holdings of most collections in France, which tend to specialize in native fabrics. ¶¶¶ For this reason I have chosen to present the textiles of France first—in chronological sequence extending from the 14th to the 20th Centuries. They cover 86 pages. ¶¶¶ These are followed by photographs of textiles made in other areas of the world, arranged alphabetically by country of origin. The largest number of these textiles are held by the Musée de l'Homme, whose cultural and ethnographic reach is wide and deep. ¶¶¶ My choice of photographs—color or black-and-white—is based principally on their graphic appeal to contemporary textile designers and only secondarily on their provenance or historical importance. It is therefore a personal selection, guided by my experience in the textile market. My aim here—as in the other volumes of this series—has been to show stimulating source material preserved in museums and available to working designers. ¶¶¶ My hope is that this photographic sampling will lead readers into the museums themselves. For nowhere else in our industrialized society can designers find so varied a source of textile art—produced by cultures that placed no premium on time.

FRANCE. One of the 67 scenes in the *Apocalypse of Angers* tapestry, woven in the 14th Century. The whole tapestry measures 353 feet in length and 14½ feet in height (two scenes high). It is the world's largest work of this kind and hangs in a special museum at the Château d'Angers. The photograph above shows three-quarters of one scene whose overall dimensions are about 5 by 8 feet. Though the tapestry was badly damaged over the centuries and the colors are faded, the details of figures and portraiture are remarkably lifelike. The *Apocalypse* set the pattern for many tapestries that followed. (123.059).

FRANCE. Another scene (detail) from the Angers *Apocalypse* tapestry. Like all scenes in this great medieval work of art, its subject was taken from the Apocalypse of John in the New Testament's Book of Revelation. The work was commissioned by Louis I of Anjou and was woven, probably in Paris, by the most famous tapestry weaver of his time, Nicolas Bataille, between 1373 and 1379. The artist who painted the cartoons with such grace and life-like fidelity was Hennequin of Bruges. The photograph above also shows three-quarters of the whole scene, which measures about five by eight feet. *(123.061)*

FRANCE. TOP. Embroidered appliqué, 15 × 30 cm. It was made towards the end of the 17th Century. *Musée des Arts Décoratifs, Paris—5540 (1159).*

BOTTOM. Compound silk with gold lamé, 53 cm. wide. Woven in Tours (Soieries Tourangelles) during the period of Louis XIII, 17th Century. Gift of Demonté, 1911. *Musée des Beaux-Arts de Tours—IH 121 (18268-3).*

FRANCE. Bed decoration of compound silk in the Style Bérain. It was woven during the second half of the 17th Century. Dimensions: 230 × 180 cm. *Musée des Arts Décoratifs, Paris—5132 (4554)*.

FRANCE. Brocaded silk woven during the first quarter of the 18th Century. It is 25 cm. wide. *Musée des Arts Décoratifs, Paris—9475 B (1392).*

FRANCE. TOP LEFT. Brocaded silk, Regency (1715-23). *Musée Historique des Tissus, Lyon—34064.*

TOP RIGHT. Brocaded Regency silk. *Centre de Documentation des Fils et Tissus, Tourcoing—61.*

BOTTOM LEFT. Brocaded Regency silk, probably from Lyon. *Musée Historique des Tissus, Lyon—32757.*

BOTTOM RIGHT. Brocaded Regency silk. *Centre de Documentation des Fils et Tissus, Tourcoing—342.*

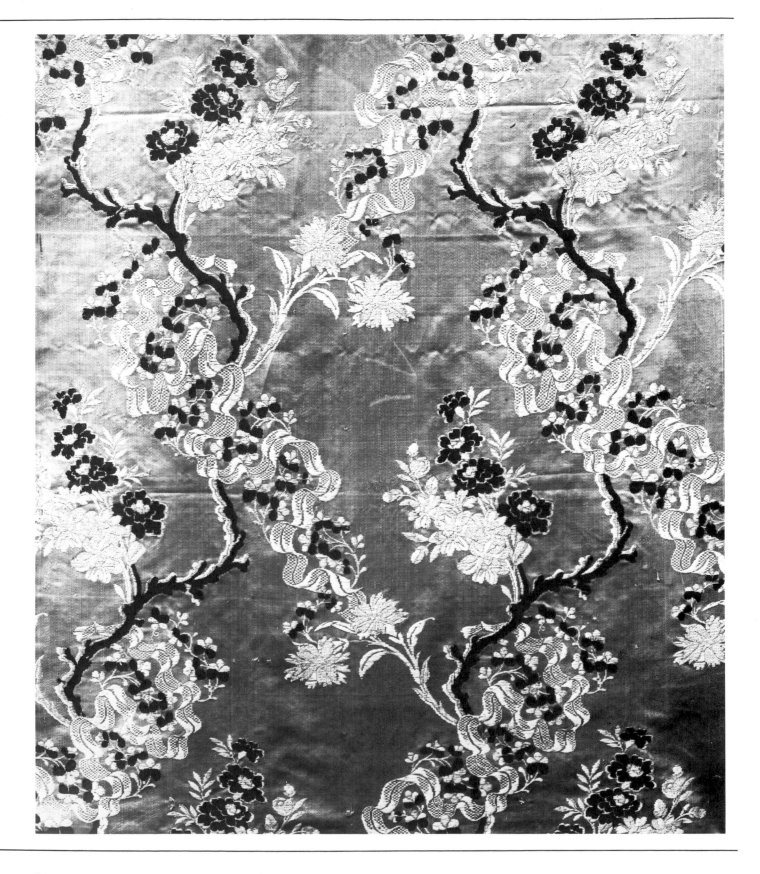

FRANCE. Brocaded satin, 55 cm. wide. Period of Louis XV (1715–74). *Musée des Arts Décoratifs, Paris—13263 (1279).*

FRANCE. Brocaded silk taffeta, 52 cm. wide. Period of Louis XV (1715–74). A piece of the same fabric is owned by the Musée Historique des Tissus in Lyon (27106). *Musée des Arts Décoratifs, Paris—12629 (1286).*

FRANCE. TOP ROW. Costume and fabric detail, dated 1750–55. The fabric is a Gros de Tours silk damask. *Musée du Costume (Carnavalet), Paris.*

BOTTOM ROW. Costume and fabric detail, dated about 1735. The silk fabric was woven by a technique known as Point Rentré, which simulates embroidery. It was invented in 1735 by a Lyon textile manufacturer called Revel. *Musée du Costume (Carnavalet), Paris.*

FRANCE. Patterned woolen fabric (droguet) woven during the Louis XV period (1715–74).
Centre de Documentation des Fils et Tissus, Tourcoing—2043.

FRANCE. Sculptured velvet, period of Louis XV (1715–74). The ground is decorated with embroidered pearls not visible in the photograph. *Musée Historique des Tissus, Lyon—2234.*

FRANCE. LEFT. Brocaded satin, Louis XV period (1715–74). *Musée Historique des Tissus, Lyon—33662.*

RIGHT. Brocaded silk, 52 cm. high, Louis XV. *Musée des Arts Décoratifs, Paris—12906 (1280).*

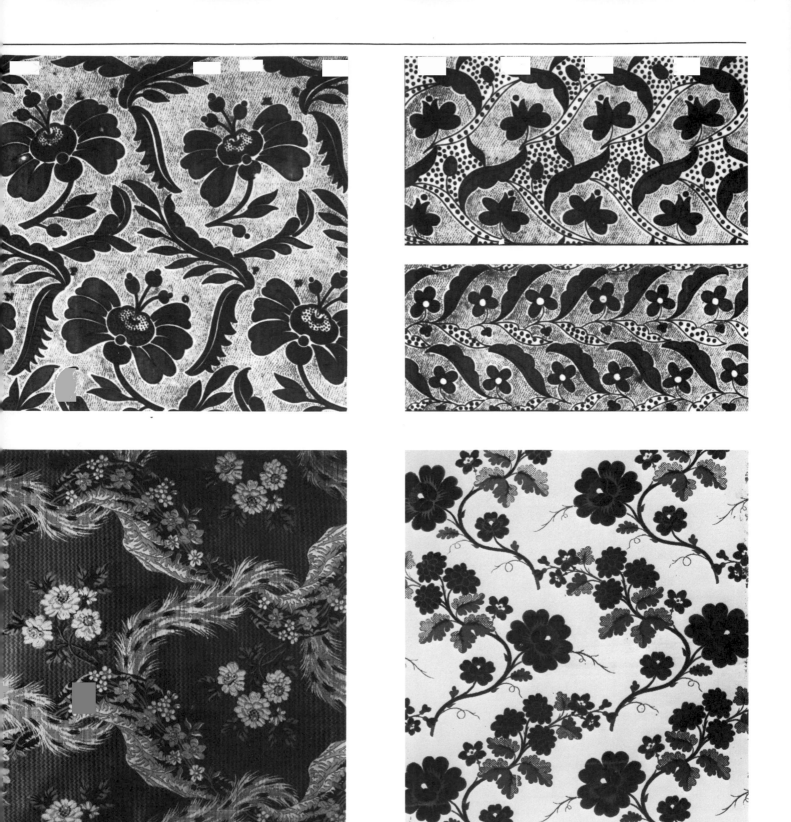

FRANCE. TOP LEFT & RIGHT. Three designs from plate 94 of the 18th-Century work by Paulet entitled *L'Art de Fabriquer les Etoffes de Soie. Musée Historique des Tissus, Lyon—C.960.*

BOTTOM LEFT. Brocaded silk, Louis XV period (1715–74). *Musée Historique des Tissus, Lyon—26071.*

BOTTOM RIGHT. Sculptured velvet, Louis XV period. *Musée Historique des Tissus, Lyon—27939.*

FRANCE. Figured compound silk, Louis XV period. *Musée Historique des Tissus, Lyon—29712.*

FRANCE. Satin chenille with brocaded figures from the period of Louis XVI (1774–93). The design is typical of Philippe de Lasalle (1723–1803), the most famous silk designer of the Lyon school. The fabric was made for Marie Antoinette at Fontainebleau. *Mobilier National—GMMP-859 (6068)* (see color section for detail of the same fabric from the Lyon museum).

FRANCE. Another example of Philippe de Lasalle's superb craftsmanship, also from the Louis XVI period. It is a brocaded satin, 55 cm. wide. Lasalle was not only the leading designer of Lyon silks. He was also an accomplished weaver who was himself able to produce the elaborate and ornate designs he created for court and nobility. *Musée des Arts Décoratifs, Paris—18493 (1363).*

FRANCE. 18th-Century Chinoiserie print in the style of Pillement, who was one of the leading artists working for the Oberkampf printworks at Jouy. This design is dated about 1785. It is 69 cm. wide. The Chinoiserie style was a pervasive influence in textile design during the late 18th Century, and Pillement was its most admired exponent. *Musée des Arts Décoratifs, Paris—25468 (6190).*

FRANCE. TOP. One in a collection of widely published drawings by Jean Pillement (1727–1808). So important was this artist's influence that his name became identified with the Chinoiserie style. Late 18th-Century patterns are often described as "in the style of Pillement." *Musée Historique des Tissus, Lyon—A 363 II, pl. 15.*

BOTTOM. Detail of embroidered panel in the Chinoiserie style, 53 cm. wide, late 18th Century. *Musée des Arts Décoratifs, Paris—13237 (1377).*

FRANCE. TOP. 18th-Century Point d'Alençon lace surplice. *Musée Historique des Tissus, Lyon—35386.*

BOTTOM. Brocaded silk with lacelike design (Décor à Dentelle) from the period of Louis XV (1715–74). *Musée Historique des Tissus, Lyon—2862.*

106

FRANCE. Another example of the Décor à Dentelle style in a woven silk. It dates from the beginning of the 18th Century and is 50 cm. wide. *Musée des Arts Décoratifs, Paris—13207 (1229).*

FRANCE. Detail from a woven silk chasuble (Décor à Dentelle), dated 1710–1720 and 58 cm. wide. *Musée des Arts Décoratifs, Paris—12908 (1262).*

FRANCE. Décor à Dentelle design in brocaded gold yarn on a violet-colored silk-damask ground. It dates from the period of Louis XV (1715–74). *Musée Historique des Tissus, Lyon—28514.*

FRANCE. This is perhaps the most famous of the Toiles de Jouy—*Les Travaux de la Manufacture*. Examples of the print are owned by many museums. This one comes from the Musée de l'Impression sur Etoffes in Mulhouse. It was designed by Jean Baptiste Huet (1745–1811) in 1783 or 1784 and is the first pattern he made for the Oberkampf printworks, where he became the star designer. It is a copperplate print showing the different methods and stages used in the preparation, printing, and finishing of textiles at Jouy. Four details from the toile are shown on the facing page.

TOP LEFT. Smoothing and rolling out the cloth. Below is the designer (Huet?) working on a pattern.

TOP RIGHT. Oberkampf and his young son; retouching colors by hand; washing the cloth.

BOTTOM LEFT. The fabric-drying house. In the foreground lengths of cloth are being stretched to shape.

BOTTOM RIGHT. The copperplate printing press with the fabric emerging on top.

FRANCE. This copperplate Toile de Jouy presents a romanticized picture of America welcoming the nations of Europe. The section shown is 93 cm. wide. Printed about 1783. *Musée des Arts Décoratifs, Paris—18614 (6186).*

FRANCE. TOP. *L'Offrande à l'Amour*—a copperplate Toile de Jouy by Jean Baptiste Huet in his earliest style, dated about 1785. The detail shown is 122 cm. wide. *Musée de l'Impression sur Etoffes, Mulhouse.*

BOTTOM. Detail from the copperplate Toile de Jouy titled: *Louis XVI—Restaurateur de la Liberté.* It was designed by Huet in the style of his second period and is dated 1788–89. The section shown is 94 cm. wide.
Musée de l'Impression sur Etoffes, Mulhouse.

FRANCE. Design on paper for a dress print. It was made at the Oberkampf works in Jouy at the end of the 18th Century. Apparel prints like this one and the three shown on the facing page were the main item of production at Jouy and other French printworks. The more famous story-telling toiles (Toiles de Jouy), generally printed only in one color, were actually only a small part of printwork production. These more colorful dress prints were the main source of income for all printworks.
Musée de l'Impression sur Etoffes, Mulhouse—S. Jouy II, p. 22-12740.

FRANCE. TOP. Another late 18th-Century Jouy design. *Musée de l'Impression sur Etoffes—p. 92-10753.*

BOTTOM. There was great variety in these Jouy prints. *Musée de l'Impression sur Etoffes—p. 95-10744.*

RIGHT. The traditional Indienne type of dress print from Jouy. Such prints were tremendously popular and were cheaper to produce than the larger toiles. *Musée de l'Impression sur Etoffes—p. 96.*

FRANCE. A heavily covered toile printed in Rouen in the 18th Century. It is titled *Le Mois de Juin*, or *J. J. Rousseau et Mme. de Warens. Musée de l'Impression sur Etoffes—954.381.1-158.*

FRANCE. TOP LEFT. Print by Huguenin l'Ainé, Mulhouse, 1785. *Musée de l'Impression sur Etoffes—314, p. 111.*

BOTTOM LEFT. Print by Pelloutier of Nantes. 1780. *Musée des Salorges, Nantes.*

RIGHT TOP & BOTTOM. Engraved woodblock and print, made in the 18th Century by the firm of Favre, Petitpierre et Cie. of Nantes. *Musée des Salorges, Nantes.*

FRANCE. Woven stain stripe (à poil traînant) from the period of Louis XVI (1774–92).
Musée Historique des Tissus, Lyon—33789.

FRANCE. Compound figured silk with a satin ground. Louis XVI period (1774–92).
Musée Historique des Tissus, Lyon—26458.

FRANCE. LEFT. Panel of gold brocade on a blue satin ground from the period of Louis XVI (1774–92). *Mobilier National, Paris—GMMP 110 (5883).*

RIGHT. Another brocaded-silk panel on a blue ground from the Louis XVI period. This piece, and the one on the left were made to furnish the royal palaces. *Mobilier National, Paris—GMMP 132 (5404).*

FRANCE. TOP. A Louis XVI satin stripe. *Centre de Documentation des Fils et Tissus, Tourcoing—1751.*

BOTTOM. A Louis XVI painted silk. *Mobilier National, Paris—GMMP 1057 (6077).*

RIGHT. Design for a woven silk border, Tours, July 1780. *Musée des Beaux-Arts de Tours—IH-204 (17553-5).*

FRANCE. Silk taffeta, warp printed (chiné à la branche). Period of Louis XVI (1774–92). *Musée Historique des Tissus, Lyon—2976.*

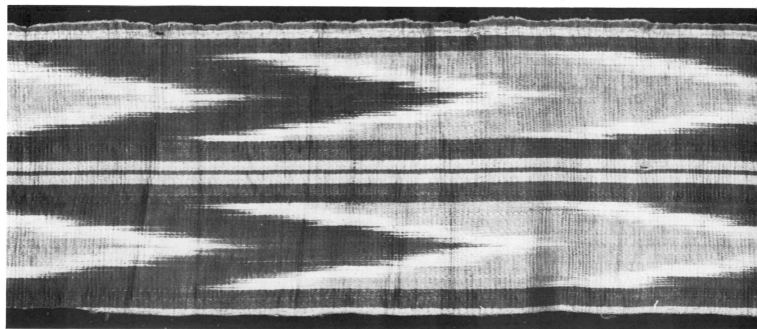

FRANCE. TOP. Another warp-printed silk taffeta, Louis XVI. *Musée Historique des Tissus, Lyon—25526.*

BOTTOM. French warp-dyed silk (Imberline chinée à la branche) with the quality of a Central Asiatic ikat. Period of Louis XVI. *Musée Historique des Tissus, Lyon—24661.*

FRANCE. Hanging of embroidered white satin from the Empire period (1804–15). Together with the matching pieces shown on the facing page it forms a coordinated set made to furnish chambers in the French royal palaces. Like other pieces in the fabulous Mobilier National collection, it is in pristine condition, since it was probably never used but was held in reserve to replace a duplicate piece that might wear out. *Mobilier National—GMMP 28 (5370).*

FRANCE. LEFT. Empire embroidered-satin seat coverings made to coordinate with the hanging shown on the left. These too are apparently unused. *Mobilier National—GMMP 33 (5399).*

RIGHT. Embroidered white satin borders made to coordinate with the Empire hanging and seat covers shown on the left. *Mobilier National—GMMP 29–30 (5530).*

FRANCE. Another resplendent hanging from a set of coordinated furnishings fabrics (see facing page) for one of the French royal palaces. The ground is crimson satin. The design is brocaded in brilliant yellow gold thread. Empire period (1804–15).
Mobilier National—GMMP 184 (5375).

FRANCE. LEFT. Gold brocaded seat covers on a crimson satin ground, designed to coordinate with the hanging shown on the left. Empire period. *Mobilier National—GMMP 195–196 (5407).*

RIGHT. This panel also coordinates with the hanging and seat covers shown on the left. The splendor of these fabrics can only be suggested in a photograph. They are truly breathtaking. *Mobilier National—GMMP 186 (5376).*

FRANCE. TOP. Border of a velvet hanging (Velours Gandin). Empire period (1804–15).
Musée Historique des Tissus, Lyon—29049.

BOTTOM. Another velvet border made for the bedchamber of the Emperor at Fontainebleau. Empire
Empire period (1804–15). *Musée Historique des Tissus, Lyon—24808-2.*

FRANCE. Woven hanging made with brocaded gold thread on a blue silk ground. Empire period (1804–15). *Mobilier National, Paris—GMMP 139 (5372).*

FRANCE. Brocaded gold on blue satin for a royal chair, designed to coordinate with the curtain and border materials on the facing page. Empire period (1804–15). *Mobilier National, Paris—GMTC 82 (5466).*

FRANCE. LEFT. Royal drapery fabric in brocaded gold on blue satin with the coronet motif that appears in the matching seat cover at left. Empire period (1804–15). *Mobilier National, Paris—GMTC 81 (5371).*

RIGHT. Border material to match the curtaining at left. *Mobilier National, Paris—GMTC 84 (5537).*

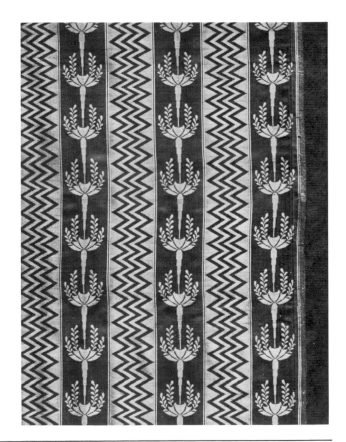

FRANCE. LEFT. Empire silk in green satin with white figures. *Mobilier National—13773 (5484).*

TOP. Empire satin lampas in blue and gold. *Mobilier National—GMMP 1045 (5299).*

BOTTOM. Woven apricot silk (Gourgouran). Empire period. *Mobilier National—GMMP 1658/3 (5284).*

FRANCE. Blue silk damask, Empire. *Mobilier National—GMMP 1658/9 (5424).*

FRANCE. LEFT. Empire gold on blue satin panel with Imperial "N." *Mobilier National—GMTC 99 (5334).*

TOP & BOTTOM. Empire chair covers to match the panel at left. *Mobilier National—GMTC 99 (5403).*

FRANCE. TOP. Empire chair cover to match the panel at right. *Mobilier National—GMMP 1392 (6955).*

BOTTOM. Another matching chair cover for the hanging at right. *Mobilier National—GMMP 1391 (6954).*

RIGHT. Figured silk hanging in white on lemon yellow. Empire period. *Mobilier National—GMMP 1391-2 (5312).*

FRANCE. LEFT. Blue satin lampas with white-lemon motifs. Empire. *Mobilier National—1048-9 (5301).*

TOP. Empire damask "Economique" in orange/white. *Mobilier National—GMT 5277 (5296).*

BOTTOM. Empire damask "Economique" in white on blue. *Mobilier National—GMMP 1374 (5346).*

FRANCE. Empire satin-ground lampas for a seat cover. *Musée Historique des Tissus, Lyon—24578/1.*

FRANCE. A graceful woven silk (lampas) produced by Schulz, Gouzolon et Cie for the Universal Exposition of 1889. Width: 59 cm. *Musée des Arts Décoratifs, Paris—5870 (1351).*

FRANCE. TOP LEFT. Silk furnishings fabric, 1896. *Centre de Documentation des Fils et Tissus, Tourcoing—80.*

TOP RIGHT. Satin damask by Audibert et Cie, Lyon, 1889. *Musée Historique des Tissus, Lyon—24955.*

BOTTOM LEFT. Silk velvet, woven in 1883. *Centre de Documentation des Fils et Tissus, Tourcoing—65.*

BOTTOM RIGHT. Sculptured velvet, made in Lyon, 1885. *Musée Historique des Tissus, Lyon—24874.*

FRANCE. Figured silk (lampa) designed by A. Martin for the firm of Mathevon, Bouvard et Cie. and exhibited at the Universal Exposition of 1878. Width: 74 cm. *Musée des Arts Décoratifs, Paris—13600 (1346).*

FRANCE. Woven silk (lampas) produced by the firm of Piotet et Rogue of Lyon and exhibited at the Universal Exposition of 1889. Width: 62 cm. *Musée des Arts Décoratifs, Paris—5868 (1348).*

FRANCE. *La Chimère*, a woven silk produced in Tours in the 19th Century and designed by Grandbarbe, a leading designer of Soieries Tourangelles. It is woven in three colors on a black ground. Dimensions of the piece shown are 55 × 62 cm. Gift of Maison Croué, 1932. *Musée des Beaux-Arts de Tours—IH 352 (294).*

NCE. Another example of the 19th-Century Soieries Tourangelles titled *L'Indien*. The weave is silk satin on ck ground, and the dimensions of the section shown are about 54 cm. square. Gift of Maison Croué, 1932. *e des Beaux-Arts de Tours—IH 348 (293).*

FRANCE. A 19th-Century design layout on paper (mise en carte), made in Tours for a woven silk and derived from a design first made at the end of the 18th Century. *Musée des Beaux-Arts de Tours—(285).*

FRANCE. LEFT. Cut velvet by Mathevon et Bouvard, Lyon, 1868. *Musée Historiques des Tissus—31403.*

RIGHT. Sculptured velvet with silk embroidery and chenille. Made by the Lyon firm of Bissardon et Bony in 1811. *Musée Historique des Tissus—26959.*

FRANCE. A woven hanging from Abbeville (Tenture d'Abbeville) made for the coronation of Charles X in 1825. Abbeville is a small village in the Somme district of Northern France and was famous for machine-woven hangings like the one shown here. They were woven, like rugs, more loosely than the traditional tapestry. *Mobilier National—(2802).*

FRANCE. A woven-silk shawl with remarkably fine lacelike detailing. It was woven during the Restoration period (1814–30) and probably in Lyon. *Musée Historique des Tissus, Lyon—24768.*

FRANCE. A pictorial toile printed in Nantes about 1825. The romantic subject is *Louis XIV and Mlle. de la Valliere.*
Musée de l'Impression sur Etoffes, Mulhouse—954.461.1.

FRANCE. TOP. Detail of *Paul & Virginia*, a Toile de Jouy printed in 1802. *Musée de l'Impression sur Etoffes, Mulhouse—461.359.1.*

BOTTOM. Detail of a Toile de Jouy whose subject is a fable of Fontaine: *The Miller, his Son, and the Donkey*. It was designed by Jean Baptiste Huet in 1806. *Musée de l'Impression sur Etoffes, Mulhouse.*

FRANCE. A cotton furnishings print made in 1853 by the Alsatian firm of Schwartz-Huguenin. *Musée de l'Impression sur Etoffes, Mulhouse.*

FRANCE. TOP LEFT. Print by Scheurer-Rott, Mulhouse, 1879. *Musée de l'Impression sur Etoffes—310, p. 15–4.*

TOP RIGHT. Print by Koechlin-Baumgartner, Alsace, 1879. *Musée de l'Impression sur Etoffes—310, p. 38.*

BOTTOM LEFT. Print by Steinbach-Koechlin, Alsace, 1877. *Musée de l'Impression sur Etoffes—524, p. 6–2.*

BOTTOM RIGHT. Print by Weiss-Fries, Alsace, 1879. *Musée de l'Impression sur Etoffes—310, p. 37–3.*

FRANCE. Section of a *Cachemire* woodblock print produced in 1863 by the Mulhouse printworks of Thierry-Mieg. *Musée de l'Impression sur Etoffes.*

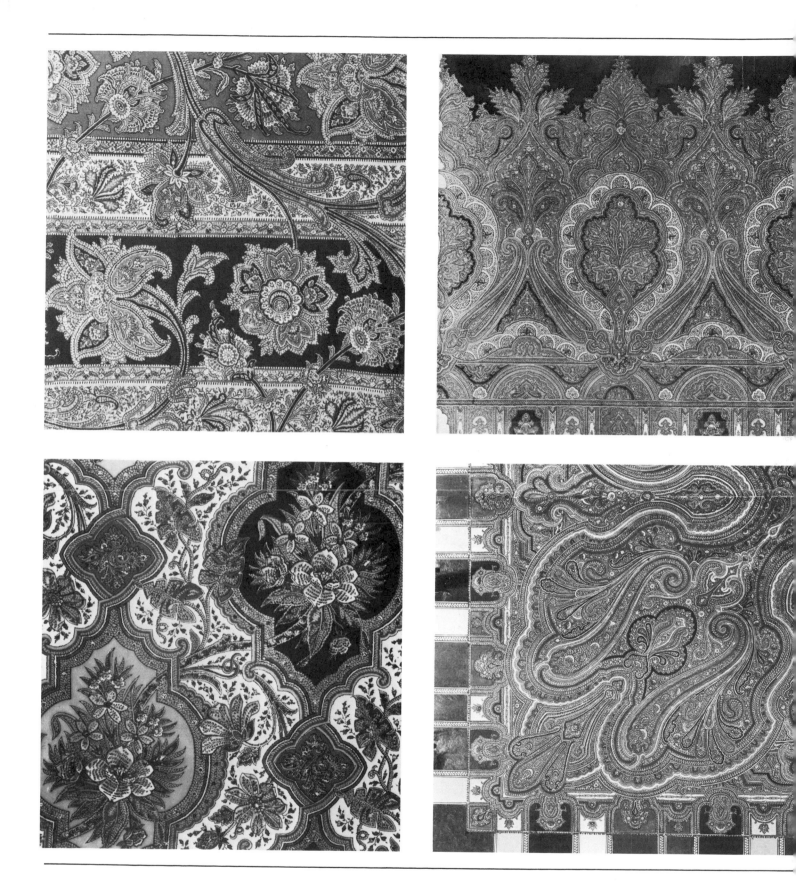

FRANCE. TOP LEFT. An Alsatian *Cachemire* print, 1870–73. *Musée de l'Impression sur Etoffes—349, p. 45-3055.*

TOP RIGHT. Printer's proof, Alsatian design, 1860–69. *Musée de l'Impression sur Etoffes—532, p. 11-3399.*

BOTTOM LEFT. Alsatian print dated 1873–76. *Musée de l'Impression sur Etoffes—350, p. 91-331.*

BOTTOM RIGHT. Printer's proof, Alsace, 1860–69. *Musée de l'Impression sur Etoffes—532, p. 38-1.*

FRANCE. Furnishings print on glazed percale made in 1853 by the Alsatian printworks of Schwartz-Huguenin. *Musée de l'Impression sur Etoffes, Mulhouse.*

FRANCE. *Monuments d'Egypte*—an early 19th-Century Toile de Jouy. It may have been designed by Jean Baptiste Huet. *Musée Historique des Tissus, Lyon—26597.*

FRANCE. TOP LEFT. 19th-Century floral print. *Centre de Documentation des Fils et Tissus, Tourcoing—2122.*

TOP RIGHT. Textile design, Atelier Schaub, Mulhouse, 1850–1900. *Musée de l'Impression sur Etoffes—40.*

BOTTOM LEFT. Another Schaub design in gouache, 1850–1900. *Musée de l'Impression sur Etoffes, Mulhouse.*

BOTTOM RIGHT. Furnishings print by Schwartz-Huguenin, Alsace, 1850–60. *Musée de l'Impression sur Etoffes.*

FRANCE. Anonymous design sketch made about 1868–71 for the firm of Stenbach-Koechlin, Alsatian printers. *Musée de l'Impression sur Etoffes, Mulhouse—528, p. 22-5.*

FRANCE. Chasuble embroidered with metallic gold thread on a satin ground. Made between 1700 and 1730. 114 × 77 cm. *Musée des Arts Décoratifs, Paris—6018A (1174).*

FRANCE. TOP. Early 19th-Century embroidery. *Musée Historique des Tissus, Lyon—19236.*

BOTTOM. Ornate embroidery for a man's coat, worked in silk thread on a silk-taffeta ground. It is from the period of Louis XVI (1774–1792). *Musée Historique des Tissus, Lyon—30915 (Wa 140).*

FRANCE. TOP. Early 19th-Century embroidery. *Musée Historique des Tissus, Lyon—35128/1,*

BOTTOM. Embroidery in silk and chenille on a satin ground from the late 18th or early 19th Century. *Musée Historique des Tissus, Lyon—35128/1.*

FRANCE. TOP. Early 19th-Century embroidery in silk thread on a striped-silk ground (Pékin). *Musée Historique des Tissus, Lyon—18624.*

BOTTOM. Another example of early 19th-Century French embroidery. *Musée Historique des Tissus, Lyon—2961/2.*

FRANCE. *La Pêche*—a printed cotton designed by Raoul Dufy for Bianchini-Férier and produced about 1920. The section shown measures about 120 cm. in height. *Musée des Arts Décoratifs, Paris—25984 (8102).*

FRANCE. *La Moisson*—another printed cotton designed by Raoul Dufy for Bianchini-Férier and also dated about 1920. The detail shown is about 80 cm. high. *Musée des Arts Décoratifs, Paris—25985 (7651).*

FRANCE. Woven-silk Crêpe Marocain with printed effects (lancé impression ad hoc). It was made about 1920, probably in Lyon. The detail shown is about 50 cm. wide. *Musée Historique des Tissus—34658.*

FRANCE. TOP. Woven-silk Crêpe Marocain enhanced with metallic yarn. It was probably produced in Lyon about 1900. *Musée Historique des Tissus—34838*.

BOTTOM. Another example of Crêpe Marocain with the addition of printed effects. It was also produced about 1920 and probably in Lyon. *Musée Historique des Tissus—34644*.

FRANCE. Woven damask produced in 1920 by the Compagnie des Arts Français from a design by André Marc. The detail shown is about 65 cm. wide. *Musée des Arts Décoratifs, Paris—21842 (8104).*

FRANCE. LEFT. Woven satin from a design by Georges de Feure, produced about 1900. The detail shown is approximately 58 cm. wide. *Musée des Arts Décoratifs, Paris—12926 (5443).*

RIGHT. *Les Fruits d'Or*—a woven satin designed by Edouard Bénédictus and produced in 1925 by Brunet, Meunié et Compagnie. Detail shown: about 53 cm. wide. *Musée des Arts Décoratifs, Paris—25953 (7652).*

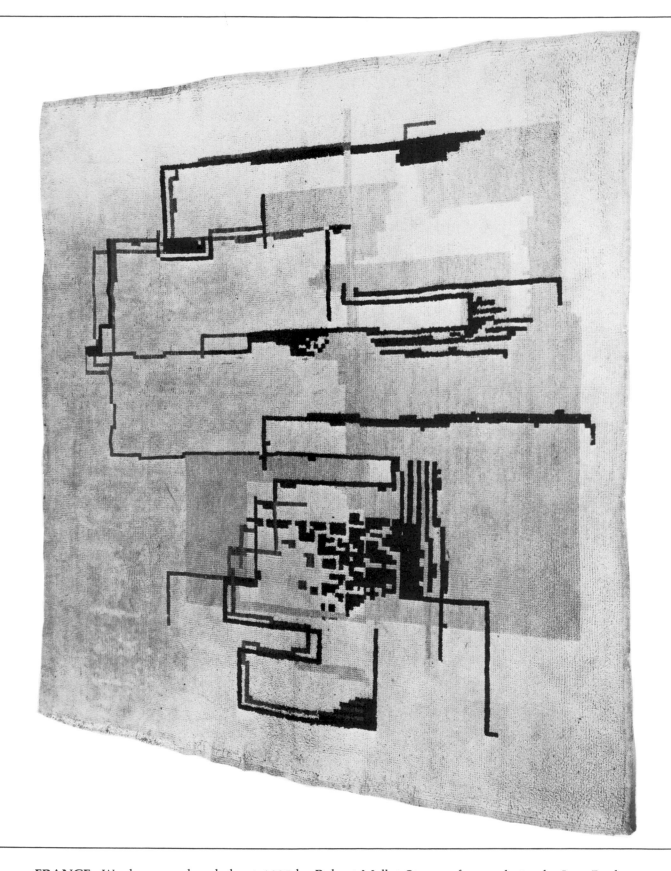

FRANCE. Wool rug produced about 1925 by Robert Mallet Stevans from a design by Jean Burkhalter. It measures 192 × 188 cm. *Musée des Arts Décoratifs, Paris—38606B (8058).*

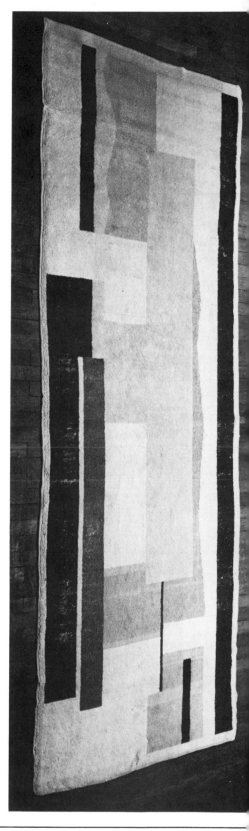

FRANCE. LEFT. Wool rug by Gustave Miklos, executed about 1925 for the studio of Jacques Doucet. It measures 156 × 85 cm. *Musée des Arts Décoratifs, Paris—38161 (7606).*

RIGHT. Wool rug designed by Fernand Léger about 1925. *Musée des Arts Décoratifs, Paris—38606A (8059).*

FRANCE. TOP. *Simultané*—a printed wool jersey designed by Sonia Delaunay in August 1926. Size is 34 × 26 cm. *Musée des Arts Décoratifs, Paris—40409 (5965).*

BOTTOM. Printed crepe de chine by Sonia Delaunay, 1926. *Musée Historique des Tissus—33703/6.*

FRANCE. Embroidered coat designed for Gloria Swanson by Sonia Delaunay and produced in 1923–4. *Musée Historique des Tissus, Lyon.*

AFGHANISTAN. A warp-ikat bed cover in a blend of cotton and silk. The irregular design results from the fact that it was assembled with remnants. Dimensions: 180 × 225 cm. The work may have been done in Russian Turkestan. *Musée de l'Homme—67.110.276 (C.68.5.493).*

AFGHANISTAN. An embroidered tray cloth worked on a violet-colored taffeta ground. It was made in the 19th Century and measures 43 × 47 cm. *Musée de l'Homme—72.12.323 (D.75.844.493).*

AFRICA—DAHOMEY. Embroidered-cotton tunic worked in red, blue, and yellow threads on white ground. Height of garment is 97 cm; width at base is 116 cm. *Musée de l'Homme—X.43.118 (E.74.1551.493).*

AFRICA—DAHOMEY. Embroidered robe of dark blue cotton. Stripes are red and white; figures in red, yellow, and blue. *Musée de l'Homme—36.21.103 (E.64.3664.493).*

AFRICA—DAHOMEY. Appliqué-cotton hanging on a yellow ground. Dimensions are 177 × 107 cm. It represents Meviaso, God of Thunder. Such panels are usually hung outside the chief's house. *Musée de l'Homme—36.21.12 (C.57.1230.493).*

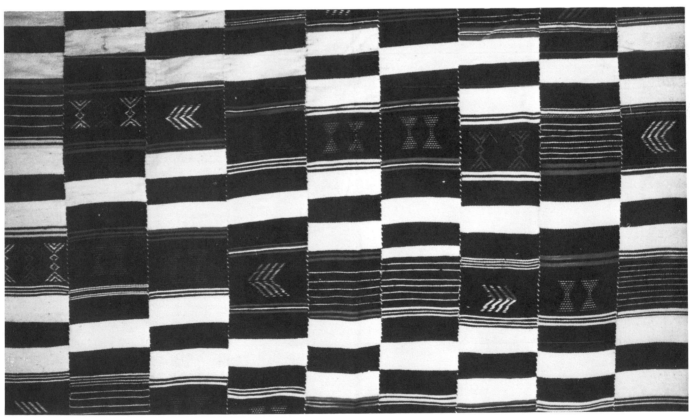

AFRICA—DAHOMEY. TOP. Detail from an embroidered-cotton hanging. The serpent measures 66 cm. and is worked in yellow, red, blue, and green. *Musée de l'Homme—30.54.913 (E.74.1541.493).*

BOTTOM. Pieced cotton cover, woven in narrow strips and then sewn together. The rectangles are blue and white with multicolored stripes. *Musée de l'Homme—D.31.4.23 (E.64.3668.493).*

AFRICA—MALI. TOP LEFT. Embroidered-cotton loincloth. *Musée de l'Homme—35.60.68 (E.64.3700.493).*

AFRICA—GHANA. TOP RIGHT. Silk Ashanti-weave Kente cloth. *Musée de l'Homme—57.3.8 (E.64.3746.493).*

AFRICA—IVORY COAST. BOTTOM LEFT. Pieced woven cotton. *Musée de l'Homme—62.59.96 (E.64.3660.493).*

AFRICA—MALI. BOTTOM RIGHT. Printed cotton, 78 cm. wide. *Musée de l'Homme—62.59.95 (E.64.3693.493).*

AFRICA—IVORY COAST. Stamp-printed cotton, 82 cm. wide. *Musée de l'Homme—64.57.1 (C.66.2099.493).*

AFRICA—NIGERIA. Loincloth woven with cotton and colored silks. The section shown is 150 cm. wide. *Musée de l'Homme—62.67.2 (C.65.4608.493).*

AFRICA—NIGERIA. TOP. Woven sash of cotton-wool, 23 × 85 cm. *Musée de l'Homme—23.1.39 (C.65.4612.493).*

AFRICA-NIGERIA. BOTTOM. Embroidered-cotton loincloth with red and black motifs on a yellow ground, woven with fine black stripes. It is 108 cm. wide. *Musée de l'Homme—61.20.5 (E.73.1966.493).*

BOLIVIA. Section of woman's shawl (103 × 94 cm.) from the Charazani region of Bolivia, N.E. of Lake Titicaca. It was woven of wool in symbolic figures that are traditional in the area. The graphic representations of similar figures, shown left and right, are by Louis Girault and appear in the 1969 Musée de l'Homme catalog *Textiles Boliviens* (supplement to Vol. 9, No. 4, *Objets et Mondes*, p. 36). *Musée de l'Homme—65.41.15 (C.67.1013.493).*

BOLIVIA. TOP. Detail of a woven wool belt, another example of traditional Charazani weaving and design. *Musée de l'Homme, "Textiles Boliviens" catalogue, p. 109.*

BOTTOM. Woven-wool shoulder bag for a man, also from the Charazani region. It measures 43 × 28 cm. The decorative bands are in white, vermilion, emerald, blue. *Musée de l'Homme—65.41.39 (D.67.1066.493).*

CAMBODIA. Panel of late 19th-Century weft-ikat work. The full design area is shown here (about 125 cm.) without the wide solid-colored borders on left and right. Colors are predominantly deep red and black, with elephants in white (see detail in color section). *Musée de l'Impression sur Etoffes, Mulhouse—954.515.1.*

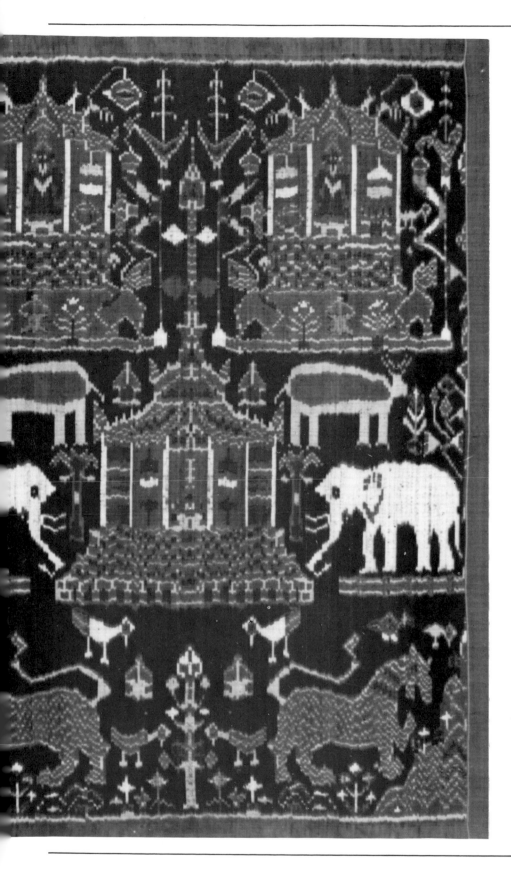

CAMBODIA. RIGHT. Section of a silk-ikat panel that was hung in the home during a marriage ceremony. It is undated but considerably more ancient than the panel on the left. The photograph shows about half the panel, which is 100 × 200 cm. overall. *Musée de l'Homme—70.61.36 (C.70.2169.493).*

CAMEROON. TOP. Section of resist-dyed cotton hanging in indigo blue and white. Overall dimensions of the piece are 188 × 135 cm. *Musée de l'Homme—35.28.1 (C.68.1548.493).*

LEFT. Enlarged detail from the same hanging. *Musée de l'Homme—35.28.1 (D.74.468.493).*

RIGHT. One end of the same hanging, 135 cm. high (the width). *Musée de l'Homme—35.28.1 (D.74.465.493).*

CAMEROON. Native-weave cotton loincloth with resist-dyed patternings of white on indigo blue. Dimensions are 165 × 216 cm. *Musée de l'Homme—62.59.100 (D.74.460.493).*

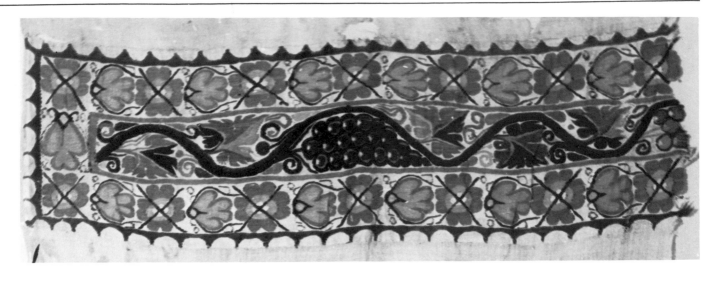

EGYPT. TOP. Tapestry-woven wool band on linen, 72 cm. wide. Coptic, 4th Century. *Louvre—Cat. A19.*

BOTTOM. Detail of a large wool tapestry panel from Antinoë, possibly woven in the 2–3rd Century A.D. (see color section for the full panel). *Musée Historique des Tissus, Lyon—28927.*

EGYPT. Coptic tapestry fragment, 5th Century. Head of a dancer, 42 × 32 cm. *Louvre—Cat. B22.*

EGYPT. TOP LEFT. 7th-Century Coptic tapestry-woven cushion cover, 77 × 65 cm. *Louvre—Cat. D131.*

TOP RIGHT. 9th-Century Coptic tapestry-woven hanging, 19 × 20 cm. *Louvre—Cat. F181.*

BOTTOM LEFT. 9th-Century Coptic *dancers* fragment, purple wool on ecru, 10 cm. wide. *Louvre—Cat. F146.*

BOTTOM RIGHT. 10th-Century Coptic tapestry-woven tunic shoulder band, 20 cm. wide. *Louvre—Cat. G238.*

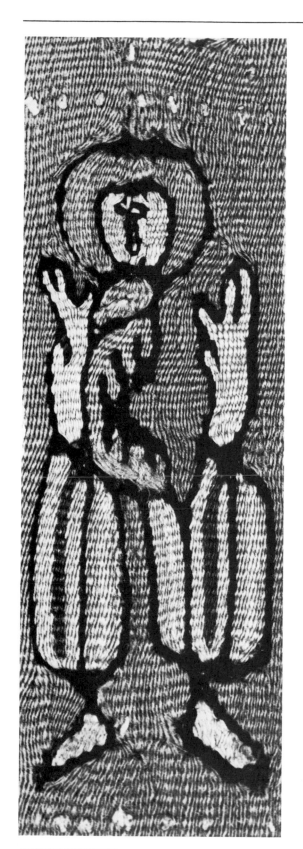

EGYPT. LEFT. 10th-Century Coptic shoulder band, detail of female dancer. *Louvre—Cat. G285.*

TOP. 11th-Century Coptic tunic shoulder band (detail). *Louvre—Cat. H190.*

BOTTOM. 12th-Century Coptic shoulder-band fragment, c. 15 cm. high. *Louvre—Cat. 130.*

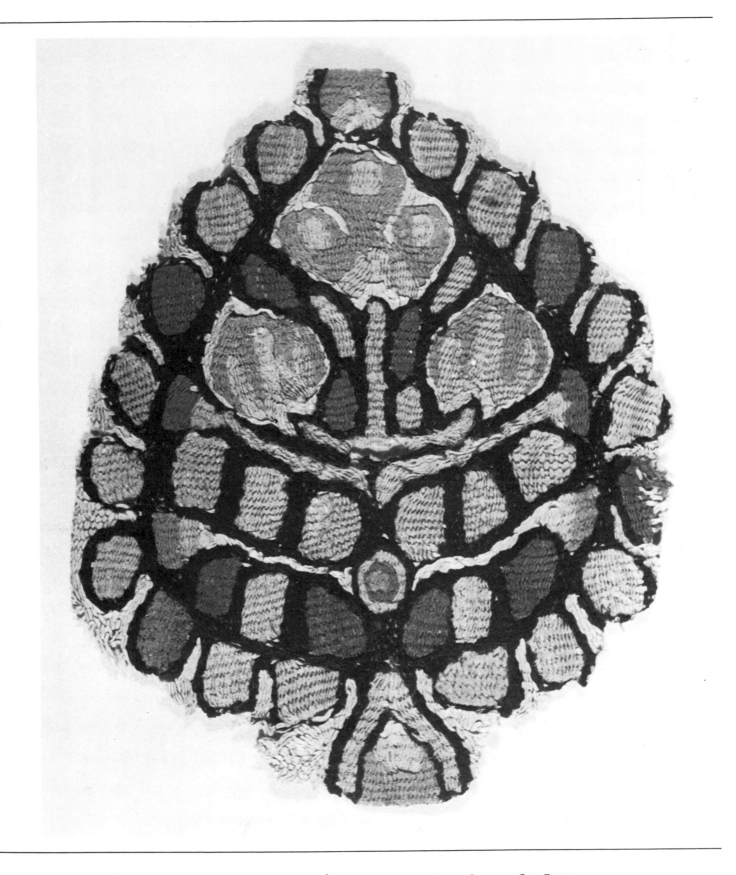

EGYPT. 8th-Century Coptic tapestry-woven fragment, 12 × 9.5 cm. *Louvre—Cat. E104.*

HUNGARY. Detail of man's apron, embroidered in silk on a satin ground, 97 × 63 cm. Acquired in 1933. *Musée de l'Homme—37.64.130 (C.64.4998.493).*

INDIA. A rare double ikat in silk. This is a marriage sari, 6 × 2 m. in size. The colors are red, green, yellow, and white on a red ground. *Musée de l'Homme—63.1.1 (C.63.552.493).*

INDIA. TOP LEFT. Child's embroidered head kerchief. Sind (?). *Musée de l'Homme—61.121.108 (C.62.631.493).*

INDIA. TOP RIGHT. Embroidery, about 140 cm. wide. *Musée de l'Homme—61.121.47 (E.62.660.493).*

PAKISTAN. BOTTOM LEFT. Woman's embroidered plaque, 41 × 38 cm. *Musée de l'Homme—64.34.8 (C.64.7034.493).*

INDIA. BOTTOM RIGHT. Detail of embroidered sash with mirrors. *Musée de l'Homme—61.121.58 (E.62.656.493).*

INDIA. TOP. Section of a painted-cotton toile, 194 × 274 cm. It dates from the 17th Century. *Musée des Arts Décoratifs, Paris—12132 (7529).*

BOTTOM. Another painted-cotton toile from 17th-Century India. Dimensions are 26 × 170 cm. *Musée des Arts Décoratifs, Paris—24932 (7667).*

196

INDIA. A painted-cotton toile from the 18th Century. The width is 159 cm.
Musée des Arts Décoratifs, Paris—27649 (6378).

INDIA. An Indo-Portuguese rug, embroidery on silk. It dates from the 17th Century and measures 278 × 188 cm. *Musée des Arts Décoratifs, Paris—22018 (5980).*

INDIA. Painted-cotton cover with the arms of the Grassin family. It was made during the first half of the 18th Century and measures 78 × 113 cm. *Musée des Arts Décoratifs, Paris—29430 (7668).*

INDONESIA. Half of a cotton weft ikat from the island of Sumba. The other half is a mirror image of the section shown. Full size of the cloth (hinggi) is 260 × 118 cm. The tortoise motif is rare. *Musée de l'Homme—61.15.5 (C.66.398.493).*

THAILAND. Section of a woven sash. It is made of cotton and silk, and the design is achieved with a supplementary yarn. It is 68 cm. wide, and the whole sash, with border, is 196 cm. long. *Musée de l'Homme—72.39.4 (D.74.1355.493).*

INDONESIA. TOP. Section of a woman's woven ritual sarong (lau) with unusual somber colorings of green and red. The design is woven with a supplementary warp. 85 cm. wide. *Musée de l'Homme—61.15.6 (C.66.400.493).*
BOTTOM. Indonesian batik in brown and indigo blue. *Musée de l'Homme—94.41.9 (C.71.330.493).*

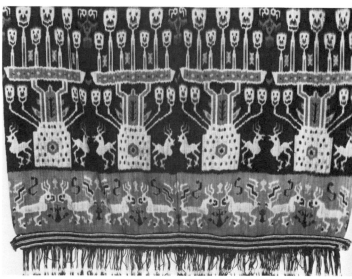

INDONESIA. TOP LEFT. Weft-ikat sarong, silk-cotton, 105 × 90 cm. *Musée de l'Homme—62.25.58 (C.63.1978.493).*

TOP RIGHT. Woman's woven ritual sarong, 70 cm. wide. *Musée de l'Homme—55.68.52 (C.66.402.493).*

BOTTOM LEFT. Section of a man's cotton ikat from Sumba. *Musée de l'Homme—55.68.60 (C.66.405.493).*

BOTTOM RIGHT. Another man's cotton ikat, Sumba, 112 cm. wide. *Musée de l'Homme—55.68.55 (C.63.1984.493).*

IRAN. Openwork hanging with embroidery and appliqué, 200 × 136 cm. It is used in religious ceremonies to separate men and women worshippers.
Musée de l'Homme—67.111.501 (C.71.814.493).

IRAN. Section of cotton tablecloth, printed by woodblock. *Musée de l'Homme—66.128.133 (C.67.2554.493).*

ITALY. Sculptured velvet from Genoa, 16th Century. The section shown is 67 cm. wide. Full length of the panel is 175 cm. *Musée des Arts Décoratifs, Paris—14614 (447).*

ITALY. Figured silk (lampas), beginning of the 17th Century. Detail shown is 53 cm. wide. *Musée des Arts Décoratifs, Paris—29459 (1194).*

ITALY. LEFT. Sculptured velvet (Velours Jardinière), 17th Century. *Musée Historique des Tissus—24683/2.*

TOP. Sculptured velvet, lamé ground, double warp. 17th Century. *Musée Historique des Tissus—21980.*

BOTTOM. 16th-Century Italian cut velvet. *Musée Historique des Tissus—22135.*

ITALY. TOP. 16th-Century embroidery (gold-silver) on satin. *Musée des Arts Décoratifs, Paris—14904 (1370).*

BOTTOM. 14th-Century figured silk (lampas) from Lucca. *Musée des Arts Décoratifs, Paris—14563 (441).*

RIGHT. Brocaded silk (gold-silver), c. 1700. 98 × 26 cm. *Musée des Arts Décoratifs, Paris—16890 (4119).*

ITALY. Fragment of a 17th-Century sculptured velvet woven in Genoa. Size is 87 × 55 cm. *Musée des Arts Décoratifs, Paris—9424 (1223)*.

ITALY. Detail of a sculptured velvet made in the 15th Century. The whole piece is 70 × 170 cm. *Musée des Arts Décoratifs, Paris—10601A (1208).*

JAPAN. Embroidered picture, probably from the 18th Century. A tour de force in silk thread on satin.
Musée Historique des Tissus, Lyon—32537.

JAPAN. Brocaded-silk serge of the 19th Century. *Musée Historique des Tissus, Lyon—23415/395.*

JAPAN. Woven-silk serge over which a central motif has been embroidered in two colors. 19th-Century.
Musée Historique des Tissus, Lyon—27175.

JAPAN. TOP LEFT. 19th-Century woven silk. *Musée Historique des Tissus, Lyon—21400.*

TOP RIGHT. 19th-Century Japanese stencil. *Musée de l'Impression sur Etoffes, Mulhouse—No. 10.*

BOTTOM LEFT. Another example of the Japanese stencil. *Musée de l'Impression sur Etoffes, Mulhouse—No. 13.*

BOTTOM RIGHT. 19th-Century Japanese stencil. *Musée de l'Impression sur Etoffes, Mulhouse.*

JAVA. Detail of a tie-dyed cotton cloth in yellow and indigo blue.
Musée de l'Impression sur Etoffes, Mulhouse.

LAOS. TOP. Detail of a woven sash in cotton and silk. The section shown is about one-half the sash and is 69 cm. wide. The design is mirrored in the other half. *Musée de l'Homme—31.42.117 (C.62.569.493).*

LAOS. BOTTOM. Embroidered cotton, 41 cm. wide. *Musée de l'Homme—32.1.592 (C.71.331.493).*

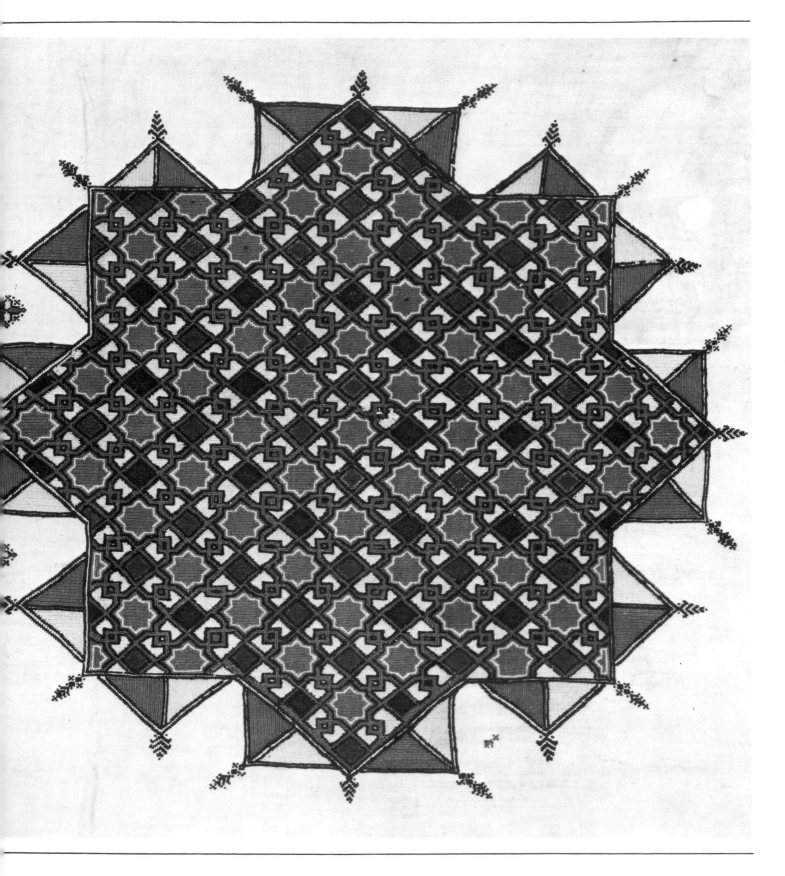

MOROCCO. Section of 18th-Century embroidery in silk threads on a linen ground. It is part of a bolster or cover. *Musée des Arts Décoratifs, Paris—16373 (3222).*

PERSIA. A silk-embroidered rug made in the 16th Century. It is 85 × 80 cm. in size. *Musée des Arts Décoratifs, Paris—16373 (3222).*

PERSIA. Woven-silk hanging, 16–17th Century. *Musée Historique des Tissus—27818.*

PERSIA. TOP LEFT. 17th-Century cut velvet, triple warp. *Musée Historique des Tissus—29340.*

TOP RIGHT. Another Persian velvet, 17th Century, single warp. *Musée Historique des Tissus—27498.*

BOTTOM LEFT. 18th-Century Persian woven silk. *Musée Historique des Tissus—Cat. 719.*

BOTTOM RIGHT. Sassanian compound silk, 7–8th Century. *Musée Historique des Tissus—24577/2.*

POLYNESIA. TOP. Tapa cloth, black design, 170 × 100 cm. *Musée de l'Homme—69.130.1 (C.72.986.493)*.

BOTTOM. Tapa cloth, brown and black design, 99 cm. wide. *Musée de l'Homme—10.9.15 (C.72.988.493)*.

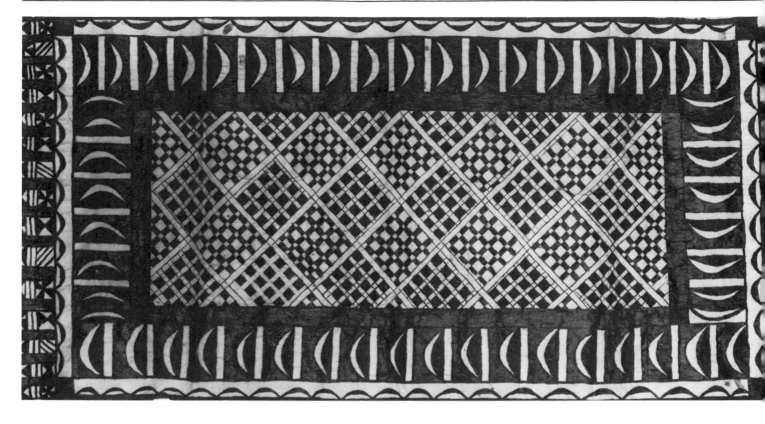

POLYNESIA. TOP. Tapa cloth, black design, 190 × 92 cm. *Musée de l'Homme—47.81.1 (C.72.990.493).*

BOTTOM LEFT. Polychrome tapa cloth, 115 × 70 cm. *Musée de l'Homme—31.60.20 (E.73.348.493).*

BOTTOM RIGHT. Section of tapa cloth, 85 cm. wide. *Musée de l'Homme—69.130.2 (C.72.993.493).*

SPAIN. An ornate 16th-Century embroidered dalmatic, worked in gold metallic thread on a velvet ground. The height is 110 cm.; width at bottom is 80 cm. *Musée des Arts Décoratifs, Paris—9411A (1161).*

SPAIN. RIGHT. The back of a 16th-Century chasuble made of sculptured velvet with woven bouclé decorations. *Musée Historique des Tissus, Lyon—27244.*

SPAIN. A 15th-Century figured silk (lampas) in the Hispano-Moresque style. Width of the section shown is about 50 cm. *Musée des Arts Décoratifs, Paris—4470 (1364).*

SPAIN. TOP. A 14th-Century Hispano-Moresque woven silk. *Musée Historique des Tissus, Lyon—28956.*

BOTTOM. A 16th-Century Spanish sculptured velvet. *Musée Historique des Tissus, Lyon—28070.*

RIGHT. A 14th-Century Hispano-Moresque lampas, 150 cm. high. *Musée des Arts Décoratifs, Paris—6019 (3306).*

TURKEY. A velvet brocaded rug with metallic silver thread. It is 114 × 64 cm. in size and was woven in the second half of the 17th Century.
Musée des Arts Décoratifs, Paris—10710 (316).

TURKEY. Section of another velvet rug (Velours Faconné), also woven in the second half of the 17th Century. It is 67 cm. wide. The full length of the rug is 123 cm.
Musée des Arts Décoratifs, Paris—4466 (305).

TURKEY. Block-printed cotton tablecloth with patterns in black. The cloth measures 136 × 82 cm.
Musée de l'Homme—973.77.111 (E.73.1938.493).

TURKEY. TOP LEFT. Gold-embroidered velvet vest, 47 × 41 cm. *Musée de l'Homme—973.77.347 (E.73.1940.493).*

TOP RIGHT. Gold-brocaded velvet, 18–19th C., 64 cm. wide. *Musée des Arts Décoratifs, Paris—14620 (307).*

BOTTOM. Embroidered hand towel, 37 cm. wide. *Musée de l'Homme—973.77.474 (E.73.1945.493).*

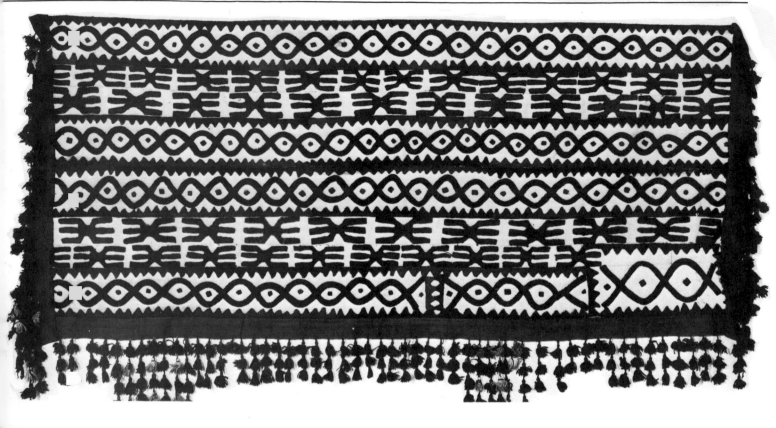

U.S.S.R. TOP. Wool-felt appliqué on cotton ground. *Musée de l'Homme—974.18.5 (D.74.527.493)*.

BOTTOM LEFT. Another wool-felt appliqué from U.S.S.R. *Musée de l'Homme—974.18.3 (D.74.525.493)*.

BOTTOM RIGHT. Hutsul embroidery from the U.S.S.R. *Musée de l'Homme—53.33.1 (C.54.1021.493)*.

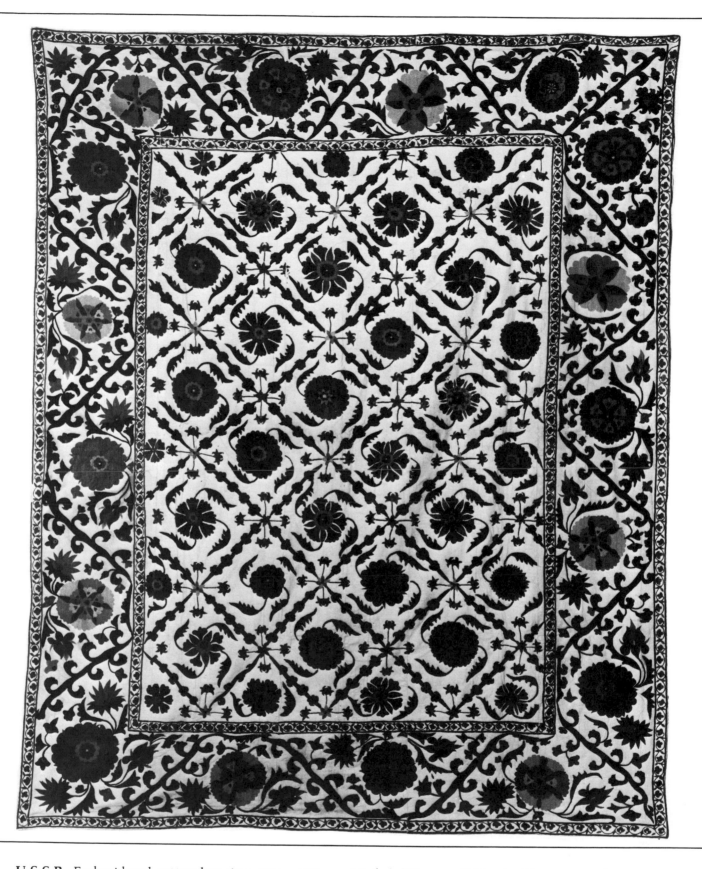

U.S.S.R. Embroidered-cotton hanging, 190 × 240 cm. *Musée de l'Homme—D62.5.80 (D.75.839.493).*

YUGOSLAVIA. The six belt details come from the Kosovo-Metohija areas of Serbia. They are women's marriage belts (Shoka), woven of wool, cotton, and metallic yarns. The width varies from 3 to 4 cm.; full length from 60 to 85 cm. *Musée de l'Homme—64.78.622-624-626-627; 55.59.526-530 (C.75.1461-1462.493).*

YUGOSLAVIA. Detail of embroidered woman's coat. The size of the motif is 55 × 44 cm.
Musée de l'Homme—55.59.452 (C.62.1054).

INDEX